The Wealthy One
(1988), a contemporary
Native American mask

Monstrous
chimera

Maori
ceremonial
adze (ax)

Hideous
Gorgon
Medusa

Ritual sword
used in Ogun
worship

Hindu animal
god Garuda

Mold and casting of Venus,
Roman goddess of love

Tibetan *vajras*,
representing
thunderbolts of
the gods

EYEWITNESS BOOKS

MYTHOLOGY

Written by
NEIL PHILIP

Maori bird-man kite

Native
American
shaman

ALFRED A. KNOPF • NEW YORK

豐川閣靈驗守護攸

Japanese
prayer
offerings

African fortune-telling
cowrie shells

Tangaroa, supreme god of Polynesia

DK

A DORLING KINDERSLEY BOOK
www.dk.com

Project editor Melanie Halton
Art editor Joanne Connor
Senior managing editor Linda Martin
Senior managing art editor Julia Harris
Production Kate Oliver
Picture research Andy Sansom
DTP designer Andrew O'Brien
Jacket designer Dean Price

This is a Borzoi Book published by Alfred A. Knopf, Inc.

This Eyewitness® Book has been conceived by
Dorling Kindersley Limited and Editions Gallimard.

www.randomhouse.com/kids

Printed in China
0 9 8 7 6 5 4 3 2 1

Library of Congress Cataloging-in-Publication Data
Philip, Neil.
Mythology / Neil Philip. — 1st American ed.
p. cm. — (Eyewitness books)
Includes index.
Summary: Surveys the treatment of gods, goddesses, the heavens,
creation, death, and evil as expressed in various mythologies around the world.
ISBN 0-375-80135-9 (trade). — ISBN 0-375-90135-3 (lib. bdg.)
1. Mythology — Juvenile literature. 2. Religions — Juvenile literature.
[1. Mythology.]
I. Title.
BL311.P485 1999
291.1'3—dc21
98-32234

Color reproduction by
Colourscan, Singapore
Printed in China by Toppan Printing Co., (Shenzhen) Ltd

Oceanic
ceremonial
ax

Staff representing
African thunder
god Shango's ax

Back of Tangaroa

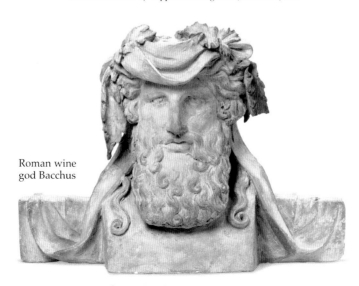

Roman wine
god Bacchus

Contents

Native American Navajo sand painting

Sand painting pigments

What is mythology?

MOTHER EARTH
This gold pendant shows Astarte, the Canaanite goddess of fertility. The great mother goddess appears in most mythologies. The Egyptian goddess Isis speaks for all: "I am Nature, the universal Mother."

THE WORD "MYTH" comes from the Greek "mythos," meaning a legend or a story. Sometimes it is used to mean something people believe that is not true: "It's a myth that carrots help you see in the dark." But mythology is not a collection of lies; it is a collection of truths. Each human culture makes stories about the creation of the world, the origins of humankind, and the meaning of life. These stories are myths. In one sense, mythology is religion in story form. But while the essence of religious belief is usually very simple, mythology can be highly complex. This is because myths are stories that explore rather than explain. They show the human mind searching to balance the forces of creation and destruction, of life and death.

Longhaired figures represent the shaman wrestling with the beaver

CREATION OF THE WORLD
Numerous mythologies tell how the creator emerged from a cosmic egg or a primordial (existing from the beginning) ocean. The world was then brought into being, perhaps from the creator's own body, perhaps from mud, or even by the power of words or thought. The first Hindu god, Brahma, is sometimes said to have been born from a golden egg that floated on the first waters.

Hindu creation symbol

Myth beginnings

Humankind has made myths from the dawn of history. The oldest living mythology is that of the Australian Aborigines, whose stories of the sacred eternal Dreamtime stretch back 40,000 years. The myths of diverse cultures are often linked by similar themes. This time line shows the approximate dates that individual societies began recording or shaping their myths.

Burning stick symbolizes the beaver's magic powers

40,000 B.C.	10,000 B.C.		4,000 B.C.	3,000 B.C.	2,000 B.C.	
Aboriginal Dreamtime tools	African god Eshu	Inuit world on a sealskin	Sumerian winged bull	Egyptian cat god Sekhmet	Chinese war god Guan Di	Aztec god Quetzalcoatl

GUIDING ANCESTORS

Ancestors play an important role in world mythology. For the Australian Aborigines, the laws and customs established by ancestor spirits (right) act as guidelines for life today. These ancestors exist outside time, in the eternal present of the Dreamtime. Aboriginal myths are stories of the Dreamtime, and Aboriginal art and ceremonies are ways of connecting with the ancestors.

The Tower of Babel fell when the workmen could no longer understand each other

CHALLENGING THE GODS

Not all are content to worship the gods; some even challenge them. When Nimrod, King of Babylon, built a tower to reach Heaven and make war on God, God sent 70 angels to confuse the builders' tongues. Some say that this is why people now speak different languages.

STORYTELLING

Myths are passed on by storytelling, not only by word of mouth and in writing, but also in rituals, dances, dramas, and artworks. This medicine beaver mask tells the story of the life-or-death struggle between a North American Nisga-a shaman, or medicine man, and a giant beaver, in which the shaman made the beaver into his spirit helper.

DEATH AND AFTERLIFE

Many mythologies hope for a new life after death. The Egyptians and the Greeks both linked the idea of an afterlife with the annual death and resurrection of corn. The Greeks worshiped Persephone (right), daughter of the corn goddess Demeter, queen of the dead, in rites that they believed held the entire human race together.

1,000
B.C.

1
A.D.

1,000
A.D.

Hindu god Garuda

Bible story of Adam and Eve

Polynesian god Tangaroa

Greek supreme god Zeus

Celtic horned god Cernunnos

Roman war god Mars

Norse god Thor's hammer

Japanese prayers

Creation of the world

MANY PEOPLES seem to agree that this world was made as a deliberate act of creation by a divine being. Often the world is described as having originally been all ocean, and it is from the sea that the world emerges in the earliest mythologies. Nun was the god of the Egyptian primal ocean. The Arctic Tikigak people say that Raven made the land by harpooning a great whale, which then floated and became dry land. Sometimes there are two creators, who together shape the world, such as First Creator and Lone Man of the Native American Mandan tribe. They sent a mud hen down to fetch mud from the bottom of the flood to make the first land.

COSMIC EGG
A bird-man from Easter Island is shown holding the cosmic egg that contains the world. Each year in the nesting season on Easter Island, the man whose servant was the first to gather an egg became the Bird Man, the living representative for that year of the creator god Makemake.

FIRE AND ICE
The Vikings believed that the world began when fire from the south met ice from the north. At the center, the ice began to thaw and, as it dripped, it shaped itself into the first being, Ymir, whose sweat formed the first frost giants. Then the ice-melt shaped a cow, whose milk fed Ymir. As the cow licked the ice, she shaped the first man, Buri.

Pottery figurine of Gaea from Thebes, 450 B.C.

FLOATING DISK
According to the ancient Greeks, the first to be born from the primeval chaos was Gaea, the Earth. The Earth was conceived as a disk floating on a waste of waters, and encircled by the river Oceanus. Gaea gave birth to Uranus, the sky, and Cronus (time).

Ahura Mazda, from the tree of life relief, 9th century B.C.

THE BIG BANG
Scientists now say that the world began with the big bang, a huge explosion 10 billion years ago that sent matter in all directions to create the ever-expanding universe. This is a new vision of beginning, a new "myth" for a scientific age.

CREATED FROM GOODNESS
The ancient Persians believed in twin spirits who had existed since the beginning of time: Ahura Mazda, who was good; and Ahriman, who was evil. It was Ahura Mazda who created the physical world, set time in motion, and created humankind.

TURTLE ISLAND

Many Native Americans believe that this world is supported on a turtle's back. According to the Seneca tribe, when the first woman fell down from another world in the sky, the toad that lived on the primal waters dived down to fetch mud to place on the turtle's back. The mud, which became Earth, provided support for the first woman.

The first land was said to have been created on a turtle's back

19th-century Native American Cheyenne shield

CURDLING OCEAN

The Japanese god Izanagi and his wife Izanami stood on the floating bridge of heaven and stirred the ocean with a jeweled spear until it curdled and formed the first island, Onokoro. They built a house there, with a central stone pillar that is the backbone of the world.

Vishnu sits on top of Mount Mandara

OCEAN CHURNING

At the beginning of this cycle of creation, a number of vital treasures, including the elixir of immortality, were not to be found, so the Hindu gods decided to churn the ocean, using Mount Mandara as the paddle. As they churned, the ocean turned to milk, then to butter, and the sun and moon arose. As they churned some more, the elixir was finally created.

Vasuki, the cosmic serpent, was used as a rope to twist the mountain

The mountain is supported by a giant turtle

The Milky Way and the planets of the Solar System. Clockwise from the bottom are the Earth, Mars, Jupiter, Saturn, Uranus, and Neptune.

The cosmos

PEOPLE HAVE ALWAYS WONDERED about the mysteries of the world, from its origin and shape to its cosmos, or order. The world is often thought to have emerged from a cosmic egg. In China, the warring forces of yin and yang in the egg created the first being, Pan Gu. The Dogon of West Africa believe the world was formed from a vibrating egg that burst open to reveal a creator spirit. The Ainu of Japan believed there were six skies above this Earth and six worlds below it, the abodes of gods, demons, and animals. The world has long been thought of as round. A myth told by the Inuit people of the Arctic tundra tells how two families set out in opposite directions to discover how big the world is. When they met up again, they were very old, but the fact that they came back to where they started proved that the world is round. The Mangaian people of Polynesia say that the universe is held in the shell of a huge coconut.

Inuit people of the Arctic tundra build an igloo, which is round like the world

WORLD IN A SEALSKIN

On this sealskin painted by the Chukchi people of Siberia, the whole world — sun, moon, land, sea, and sky — is captured in a small space. In this sealskin world, human beings share creation with spirits, animals, and gods such as the creator Raven and his wife, Miti, and Sedna, the mother of the sea beasts.

YIN AND YANG

The Chinese believed that the first being, Pan Gu, was created inside a cosmic egg by the opposing forces of yin and yang. When at last the conflict between yin and yang broke the egg open, Pan Gu was born and pushed the sky away from the Earth. After he died, exhausted by this labor, his body formed the mountains and the land — and his fleas became humankind.

Yin and yang symbolize universal opposites, such as good and evil, that must be equally balanced for a harmonious world

Brahma, the creator of the Universe, is shown on Vishnu's forehead

Vishnu's conch shell symbolizes the very first vibration of the Universe — the sound "om"

The discus symbolizes the mind and the sun

WORLD TREE

For the Vikings the nine worlds, including humankind's "middle Earth," were arranged in three layers around the huge ash tree Yggdrasil, which stands at the center of the cosmos. The Vikings believed that the worlds of gods, giants, elves, dwarfs, humans, and the dead were all sustained by the world tree.

COSMIC STONE

This Babylonian boundary stone shows the gods and goddesses of the Babylonian cosmos as witnesses to a legal agreement. At the top are symbols of the goddess of love and war Ishtar, the moon god Sin, and the sun god Shamash. An underworld snake wriggles up the side. The scorpion in the center row is the symbol of Ishhara, the goddess of marriage and childbirth and enforcer of oaths.

Sin, the moon god, is represented by a crescent moon

This symbol for the planet Venus represents Ishtar, goddess of love and fertility

Vishnu's lotus flower is a symbol of purity

NUT AND GEB

The ancient Egyptians thought that the Earth was male, personified by the Earth god Geb, and that Geb mated with his sister Nut, the sky, to produce the stars. Nut and Geb were wrenched apart by their fatherShu, god of the air, who holds Nut aloft and pins Geb down with his feet.

Each night the sun god Ra is swallowed by Nut, to be born again next morning

Underworld snakes writhe in the lowest region of the cosmos, Tala, where murderers are reborn

Watchful eyes of the owl Koururu, sacrificed by Rongo, god of agriculture, to protect his house

Varuna, god of the waters, sits on an imaginary beast

This carving stood at the entrance to a Maori assembly house on North Island, New Zealand

This golden mace is a symbol of knowledge

PAPA AND RANGI

The Maoris tell how Papa, the Earth goddess, coupled with Rangi, the sky god. So closely did Papa and Rangi cling to each other that their children could not leave the Earth womb. Eventually, Papa and Rangi were forced apart by one of their children, Tane, the forest god.

VISHNU'S WORLD

Vishnu the preserver is one of the three great gods of the Hindu religion. At the end of each cycle of creation, Vishnu sleeps on the world serpent Shesha, preserving the seed of a new creation that will rise when he wakes. When Vishnu was incarnated as the hero Krishna, his mother looked into his mouth and saw the whole universe. This 19th-century painting shows Vishnu as the universe.

Sun and Moon

THE SUN AND THE MOON, which light up the sky by day and night and enable us to tell the time, have been the subject of many myths. For the Native American Zuni people, Moonlight-Giving Mother and Sun Father are the givers of light and life. The Native American Cherokees say the sun is female and tell of her grief when her daughter died from a rattlesnake bite. Sun hid herself away, the world grew dark, and her tears caused a flood. Only the dancing and singing of young men and women could cheer her up. The Arctic Chukchi tell how a woman married the sun, but a black beetle took her place; it was only when her son sought out his father that the imposter was discovered. Another Chukchi woman married the moon; she had been deserted by her husband and left to starve, but she crawled to moon's house and became his wife.

DEALER OF DAYS
The moon god Thoth was in charge of the Egyptian calendar, which had 12 months with 30 days each. The sky goddess Nut, who had been cursed so that she could never give birth, won five extra days from Thoth in which she had her children.

THE ROMAN MOON GODDESS DIANA
Diana (Artemis in Greek) is shown here with her foot resting on the moon, with which she was closely associated. More often, however, she is depicted with a crescent moon in her hair.

Diana as a crowned moon goddess

The face on this Inuit mask represents the spirit of the moon

Decorative feathers represent the stars

White border around the face symbolizes air

Painted moon face sculpted in wood

Native American Haida mask

FEEDING HUMANKIND
The Inuit moon man is called Igaluk or Tarqeq. Shamans make spirit journeys to ask him to promise that he will send animals for men to hunt. The moon man also helps the souls of the dead to be reborn as humans, animals, or fish.

POLLUTING THE WORLD
A Native American Haida myth tells how Wultcixaiya, the son of the moon, rescued his sister from her unhappy marriage to Pestilence. Wearing a steel coat, he broke into Pestilence's house of rock, freeing her, but also polluting the world with sickness and disease.

RA, THE SUN GOD
The falcon-headed god Horus joined forces with the Egyptian sun god Ra and became Ra-Horakhty. He sailed a special boat, the "solar bark," across the sky by day and through the underworld by night.

The sun's rays beam down on a worshiper

Projections symbolize the sun's rays

INCA INTI
Viracocha, the Inca creator god, ordered the sun, moon, and stars to emerge from the Island of the Sun, in Lake Titicaca, to bring light to the world. Inti, the sun god, was regarded as the father of the Inca emperors, and his wife, Mama Kilya, the moon goddess, as the mother of the Inca race.

Pre-Columbian gold sun mask, 300 B.C.

Tsimshian chief's ceremonial headdress representing the sun

CHILDREN OF THE SUN
The Native American Tsimshian hero Asdiwal was a great hunter, who pursued a bear right up to the sky. The bear turned out to be the sun's beautiful daughter, whom Asdiwal married. The sun also has a son, a shining prince of the sky, who had a constant battle of wits with his cheeky servant.

The fertility goddess Ishtar

Ea, the water god

Shamash rising between two mountains

Amaterasu holds the imperial sword and necklace

ENEMY OF DARKNESS
The Babylonian sun god Shamash was the only being able to cross the ocean of death, until the hero Gilgamesh. Shamash was a lawgiver and healer, the enemy of darkness, wrongdoing, and disease.

THE SUN GODDESS AMATERASU
The Japanese sun goddess Amaterasu was so offended by her brother Susano's practical jokes that she hid in a cave and deprived the world of the sun. Uzume, the goddess of mirth, did a striptease and made the other gods laugh. Intrigued, Amaterasu emerged from the cave, returning sunlight to the world.

Making humankind

SNAKE GODDESS
Nü Wa, the first Chinese goddess, had the face of a girl but the body of a snake. She was lonely, so she made the first human beings out of mud and water to cheer herself up.

ALL MYTHOLOGIES TELL how the first human beings were made. Often the creator shaped them from clay or mud. The Unalit (North Alaskan Inuit) say that the first man was born from the pod of a beach pea. When he burst out of the pod, he was met by Raven, who taught him how to live and made him a wife out of clay. The Egyptians believed that the first human beings were made from the tears of Ra, the sun god. For the Serbians, people were made from the creator's sweat, which is why they say we are doomed to a life of toil. The Norse god Odin made the first man and woman from driftwood, but there is also a myth telling how the Norse god Heimdall fathered the various kinds of men: serfs, warriors, and kings.

Brahma has four heads so that he can see in all directions

BRAHMA THE CREATOR
The Hindu creator Brahma is the universal soul, the "self-existent great-grandfather." He made the world and everything in it. He is sometimes called Purusha, the first being. As Purusha he divided himself into two, male and female, and coupled in the form of every creature, from humans to ants.

Carved wooden bowl from the Yoruba in West Africa

The cosmic serpent Aido-Hwedo coiled itself around the Earth

BODIES OF CLAY
The West African creator Mawu made the first people from clay and water. The first man and woman, sometimes called Adanhu and Yewa, were sent down from the sky with the rainbow serpent Aido-Hwedo. For the first 17 days it did nothing but rain; the man and woman did not speak but only called out the name of the god who had sent them to Earth.

Adanhu

Yewa

Tangaroa brings forth other beings

Wooden statue from the Tubuaï Islands in Polynesia, where the supreme god Tangaroa is called A'a

16

Wooden idols

FIRST HUMANS
When the statue of Tangaroa (left) was first discovered, it contained wooden idols like these, which represented the first men and women.

New beings crawl on Tangaroa's back

POTTER'S PEOPLE
The Egyptian ram-god Khnum was the potter who shaped each human being and their ka, or life force, on his potter's wheel. He was worshiped at the island of Elephantine, with his wife, Satet, and their daughter Anuket, the huntress. An inscription on a block of granite found at Elephantine records how prayers to Khnum brought to an end a seven-year famine.

Tangaroa's body cavity contained wooden idols

The tree of the knowledge of good and evil

WOODEN STATUES
Tangaroa (Ta'aroa) is the Polynesian god of the ocean. In some places he is considered the maker of all things. In Tahiti it is said that Tangaroa lived inside the cosmic egg at the beginning of time. When he broke out, he called, "Who's there?" but there was no reply. So Tangaroa created the world and called forth gods and humans from his body.

Tangaroa creates other gods and humankind

ADAM AND EVE
According to the Bible, God created Adam, the first man, in his own image. He shaped him out of clay and made Eve, the first woman, from one of Adam's ribs to be his companion. Islamic tradition says that when God breathed life into Adam's nostrils, he sneezed and said, "Praise be to Allah."

17

Supreme beings

Thunderbolts were made for Zeus by the Cyclopes, giants who helped in the war against Zeus's father

M OST MYTHOLOGIES tell of one god who reigns supreme over all others. These supreme gods may be associated with the creation of the world and humankind. Many supreme deities, such as the Greek god Zeus, are essentially sky gods; others may be sun, battle, city, or tribal gods. In some cultures, especially in Africa, the supreme god is thought to have retired from the world after the initial creation. This is the case with Nana-Buluku, the creator deity of the Fon of West Africa; and with Nyame of the West African Ashanti people. Over time such gods may be almost forgotten. For instance, Nana-Buluku's daughter Mawu is now routinely described as the creator, and the word "mawu" has come to mean "god" in Fon.

Made of bronze and decorated with silver, this late Bronze Age figure represents the storm god Baal

RULER OF THE GREEKS
Zeus (known as Jupiter to the Romans) was ruler of the Greek gods. Zeus overthrew his father, Cronos, before establishing his rule on Mount Olympus. His wife, Hera, goddess of marriage, was jealous because of his many love affairs, during which he fathered the gods Apollo and Artemis, and the heroes Perseus and Heracles (or Hercules).

THE RAINMAKER
The Canaanite storm god Baal made thunder with his mace and produced lightning from his lance. Baal revolted against El, his father, by defeating El's favorite, Yam, the god of the sea. Another myth tells of his long battle against Mot, god of death.

The feathers of more than 250 quetzal birds make up this headdress

BABYLONIAN KING OF THE GODS
This doglike dragon is the symbol of Marduk, the Babylonian king of the gods. Strong and heroic, he was given authority over the other gods, including his father, Ea, the god of wisdom, when he agreed to slay the dragon Tiamat (one of two primal beings). Marduk created humankind from the blood of Tiamat's son Kingu.

FEATHERED SERPENT
Half-snake, half-bird, Quetzalcoatl was the Aztec lord of life and god of the winds. He descended to the underworld to retrieve the bones of early humans in order to create new beings. The underworld was ruled by his father, the death god Mictlantecuhtli.

Aztec serpent god Quetzalcoatl

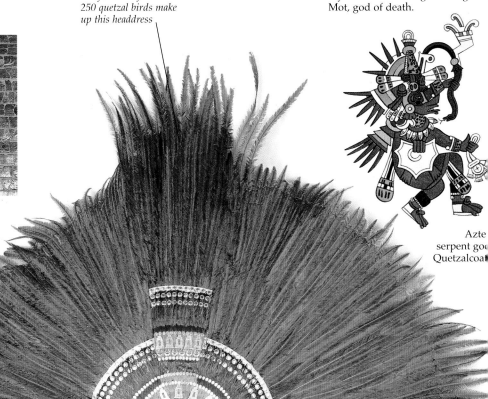

Headdress of Montezuma II, the last Aztec ruler

Wooden kantele from Karelia in Finland, 1893

Stoneware Taoist shrine of the Ming dynasty, 1406 A.D.

Lao-tzu, the founder of Taoism, is shown riding a buffalo

SINGING SHAMAN
Vainamoinen, the eternal singer, was the son of the Finnish air-goddess Ilmatar. He was born old, so no one wanted to marry him — one girl, Aino, even became a mermaid rather than be his bride. Vainamoinen was a shaman, whose songs to the sound of his harplike kantele were acts of creative magic.

The Jade Emperor

LORD OF THE HEAVENS
The Chinese gods formed a huge bureaucracy, at the head of which was the Jade Emperor. He was assisted by the God of the Eastern Peak, who had no fewer than 75 departments under his control, each supervised by lesser gods. The Jade Emperor's wife was Xi Wang Mu, the Queen Mother of the West, guardian of the peaches of immortality, which she serves at a great feast once every 1,000 years.

Ebony mortar and pestle from Tanzania, East Africa

Mortar

Pestle

The God of the Eastern Peak

STAIRWAY TO HEAVEN
Nyame is the sky god of the Ashanti of Africa. He used to live close to humans, but when an old woman annoyed him by knocking him with her pestle as she pounded yams, he moved away toward the heavens. The old woman and her sons tried to reach him by piling mortars on top of each other, but they were one short. They took the mortar from the bottom to place it on the top, and the pile collapsed, killing them all.

Floods and storms

THE STORY OF A GREAT FLOOD that once overwhelmed the Earth – a flood that only a lucky few survived – is one of the most widespread of all myths. The earliest flood story is found in the Mesopotamian epic of Gilgamesh, in which Utnapishtim frees birds to see if the waters are subsiding. The Native American Mandan tribe spoke of Lone Man, who survived a great flood in his big canoe. The Greek god Zeus, tired of the wickedness of humans, sent a flood to drown them all. But the giant Prometheus warned his son Deucalion, who built an ark in time to save himself and his wife.

SAVED BY A FISH
One day the Hindu sage Manu found a fish in his washing water. The fish told Manu that he should build a ship because a great flood was coming. When the flood arrived, the fish, which was an incarnation of the Hindu god Vishnu, towed Manu to safety. Manu then became the father of all humankind.

Giant Wave, a print of a tsunami (huge, violent wave) by Katsushika Hokusai (1760–1849)

A tsunami is usually caused by an earthquake or a volcano; here, a tsunami batters a Japanese plank boat

KINGDOM OF ATLANTIS
Poseidon, the Greek god of the sea, fell in love with a woman called Clito and built her a paradise island. Clito bore Poseidon sons, who founded the kingdom of Atlantis on the island. The brothers ruled the island in wisdom. But later rulers became greedy and corrupt, so Poseidon sent a tidal wave to swallow up Atlantis and all its people.

Headdress of tropical bird feathers

Type of poncho worn by Sapa Incas, the first of whom named himself after the supreme god Viracocha

In his left hand, Chac carries a bowl; in his right, a ball of smoking incense

MAYAN RAINMAKER
Chac, the rain god, broke open a great rock to uncover the first corn plant. And it was Chac who sent the rain each year to enable the corn to grow. But sometimes, instead of gentle rain, Chac sent violent storms, in which he wielded his weapon, lightning.

GIANT WAVES
The great flood is caused either by a deluge of rain, as in the Noah story (below), or by a gigantic tidal wave that sweeps over the land, as in the story of Atlantis (above). Both are terrifying images of unstoppable destruction.

CREATOR OF HUMANS
Viracocha, the Inca creator god, was displeased with his first attempt at creating humans from stone, so he drowned them all in a flood. He then tried again, this time making the people from clay. He wandered among these new people as a beggar, teaching them how to live.

NOAH AND THE ARK
When God saw how wicked humans had become, he decided to drown them all, for he was sorry he had ever created them. But he decided to save one good man, Noah. He warned Noah to build an ark in which to save his family and two of every living creature to people the Earth after the great flood. When the flooding subsided, God set the rainbow in the sky as a promise that he would never again destroy humanity by a flood.

Some believe that gods live at the peak of Mount Fuji in Japan, which is always capped with snow

The elements

ALL OVER the world, the elemental forces that form it have been the focus of myth-making. Fire, air, earth, and water are the "four elements" in Western tradition. The Chinese have five elements: wood, fire, earth, metal, and

Feather tassel

water. Almost all mythologies tell how humans acquired the gift of fire, often stolen from the sun. Gods of the air and the sky have been so important that the names of many supreme gods, such as the Greek Zeus, simply mean "sky." The Earth, though sometimes regarded as male, is more often thought of as our mother. According to the mythology of ancient Babylon, in the beginning nothing existed but Apsu, the freshwater ocean; and Tiamat, the saltwater ocean. These two waters have given and taken life since the dawn of time.

Agni's stomach is full because fire devours everything

FIRE-EATER
Wherever a fire is lit, the Hindu fire god Agni is born. Because he is present in all homes, he knows all secrets. He once helped a man find his wife, who had been carried away by the sage Bhrigu. Bhrigu then cursed Agni, making him consume all the dirt of the Earth. But as Agni devours the dirt, he also purifies it with his flames.

VOLCANIC PELE
In Hawaii, which is dominated by the Kilauea volcano, Pele is worshiped as the goddess of fire. She is as passionate and dangerous as a volcano. She fell in love with the prince of Kauai, but when he preferred her sister, she encased him in molten lava and turned him to stone.

OCEANS OF OLOKUN
Olokun, the sea king of the Edo people of Benin, Nigeria, is a powerful god. He is the source of all wealth and the bringer of children, whose souls must cross the ocean to be born. His palace is a paradise, full of the noise of children, and his wives, who are the rivers. The Olokun river is the source of all the waters of the Earth, including the ocean.

Mother-of-pearl eyes embedded in a painted face

Kite is made of canvas and twigs

SKY MAN

Tawhaki, the great Polynesian hero whom the Maori call the god of thunder and lightning, ascended to the sky world as a kite, seeking to avenge his father, Hema, whose eyes had been gouged out by goblins to use as lights. Maori priests foretold the future by watching the dance of kites in the air.

Balls of rolling thunder

The thunder god is depicted as a demon in the air

Maori kite in the form of a bird with a human head

Drumstick makes the thunder

EARTH MOTHER

Toci, mother of the gods, was an important Aztec earth goddess. She was a goddess of the harvest, of childbirth, and of curing, but also of war and discord. The Earth itself was said to have been made by the gods from the body of the fearsome goddess Tlaltecuhtli, who could be appeased only by being given human hearts to eat.

Aztec earth goddess (A.D. 1300–1521)

Poseidon's trident, a three-pronged fisherman's spear

THUNDER ROLLS

This burly Japanese god (possibly Kami-Nari, the god of rolling thunder) beats out thunder on his drum. Japanese thunder deities are threatening forces. When Izanagi, the primal male, descended to hell in search of his wife, the decomposing goddess sent eight thunder gods to chase him from the underworld.

Aboriginal stone ax from Northern Territory, Australia

STORMY SEAS

Poseidon, the Greek god of the sea, had a violent and vengeful nature. This showed in his persecution of the hero Odysseus, who had blinded the god's son. As well as causing storms at sea, Poseidon was also believed to cause earthquakes.

Japanese thunder god

LIGHTNING MAN

The Lightning Brothers are important ancestor figures in the Dreamtime of the Aborigines of Australia's Northern Territory. Tcabuinji killed his younger brother, Wagtjadbulla, with a stone ax in an argument about Tcabuinji's wife. It is this ax that Tcabuinji uses to split trees when lightning strikes.

The natural world

ALL THE ELEMENTS OF THE NATURAL WORLD — animals, flowers, plants, and trees — are the gifts of the gods and remain in their care. Many cultures worshiped the Earth as a mother goddess, provider of food and fertility. But they also gave responsibility for important crops — such as maize for Native Americans, or rice for the Japanese — to specific gods or goddesses. Hunting societies believe that game is withheld or released by divinities such as Sedna, the North American Inuit mistress of the sea beasts. In the forests of northern Cameroon, hunters pray to the Bedimo, ancestral spirits, to release game from their divine stables.

Spanish reed

This type of reed has been used to make pipes for 5,000 years

PAN'S PIPES
With his goatlike horns and legs, Pan was the Greek god of the pastures, especially of sheep and goats. He could inspire fear in his enemies, who would flee in what we now call a "panic." Pan was also very amorous. One nymph, Syrinx, turned into reeds to escape him. But Pan made himself a set of musical pipes from the reeds so that she would always be close to him.

Cobs of corn

SPRINGTIME GOD
The Aztec god of spring, Xipec Totec, allowed his skin to be flayed (peeled off) in order to promote new growth from within — like a corn seed breaking through its husk to become a new plant. At festivals in his honor, young men wore the skins of human sacrificial offerings.

Farmers harvesting rice

RICE SUPPLIES
Every village in Japan has a shrine dedicated to the rice god Inari, who comes down from his mountain home in the spring and returns in the autumn, after the rice harvest.

Rice grains

Wooden mask representing
the nature spirits of the
North American Inuits

Kelp
seaweed

MOTHER OF SEA BEASTS
Sedna, the Inuit sea woman,
was thrown into the sea by
her father because she married
a dog. When she tried to cling
to the kayak (boat), he chopped
off her fingers, which turned
into the first sea mammals. To
show her appreciation for the
help given her by humans,
who comb her hair, Sedna
releases the sea beasts so
that humankind can feed.

*Mask represents the various sea
beasts, such as seals and fish,
that Sedna watches over*

*This Maori ceremonial
adze (axlike tool)
symbolizes Tane, who
was himself shaped by
craftsmen with adzes*

TANE OF THE TREES
The Oceanic forest god Tane
lived in the highest heaven,
from which he brought down
three baskets of knowledge for
humankind. He made himself a
wife, Hine-hau-one (the Earth-
formed maiden), from red
sand. Their daughter, the
dawn maiden, ran away to
become Hine-nui-te-Po,
the goddess of death.

*Flora awakens
the flowers
with her
sweet music*

FLOWERING FLORA
Flora was the Roman goddess of the
flowers, who made plants and trees
bloom. Flora also had a flower which
made women pregnant when they
touched it. She lent the flower to the
goddess Juno, who soon became
pregnant with Mars, the god of war.

Celtic bronze horse found in the tomb of a prince (c. 5th century B.C.)

EQUESTRIAN EPONA
Epona, the Celtic horse goddess, is closely linked to the triple mother goddesses, who are often shown nursing babies. Like them, Epona is often shown with wheat and other fertility symbols, but she was especially associated with horse breeding. Horse breeding was crucial because the Celts farmed with horses, and without them could not have grown enough food.

Fertility and birth

WORSHIP OF THE GREAT MOTHER goddess, often identified as the Earth, has been part of many religions since the dawn of humanity. For instance, Pacha Mama, the name of the Inca fertility goddess, means "earth mother." When the Hittite god of farming, Telepinu, withdrew from the world in a rage, and humans began to starve, it was the mother goddess Hannahanna who found him. The myth of the Greek corn goddess Demeter and her despairing search for her lost daughter Persephone, during which the Earth became a wasteland, was at the heart of Greek religion. Birth and fertility were not exclusively the reserve of goddesses. Frey was the Norse god of fertility, a role given in Egypt to the gods Min and Osiris; Egyptian mothers wanted the aid of the impish god Bes at childbirth.

FREY AND FREYA
Twin brother and sister Frey and Freya were Norse fertility gods. Frey's cult involved his image being carried from place to place in a wagon during the winter months to ensure fertility. Freya, who was considered to be the most beautiful of all goddesses, was primarily the goddess of love and of soothsaying (predicting the future).

Frey holds his beard, a symbol of growth, in one hand

Goddess Freya in her chariot

JADE SKIRT
Chalchiuhtlicue, "she of the jade skirt," was the central Mexican goddess of lakes and streams and, by association, the goddess of birth. She is sometimes depicted with a pair of babies, one male and one female. Chalchiuhtlicue once flooded the Earth but turned humankind into fish so that they were saved.

The water goddess Chalchiutlicue stands in water near a giant centipede

26

Native American Iroquois corn husk mask, worn in midwinter ceremonies to ensure a good harvest

Alabaster figurine of Ishtar c. 300–200 B.C.

Baby Horus

LOVE GODDESS
Ishtar, the Babylonian goddess of love, descended to the underworld to rescue her dead husband Tammuz, god of plants. But she was killed and, without Tammuz, the whole world withered. Ishtar was brought back to life, but for six months of each year Tammuz must live in the underworld, while Ishtar laments; when he rises in the spring, all rejoice.

ISIS AND HORUS
The Egyptian goddess Isis is often shown as the perfect mother, nursing the infant Horus. When he was only a baby, Horus was bitten by scorpions and would have died, but Isis's cries of anguish halted the sun god Ra in his journey across the sky. Ra then sent the god Thoth to cure the child.

FIRST MOTHER
Native Americans of the Northeast tell how First Father was born from the foam on the sea, and First Mother from the dew on the leaf. The human race increased, but eventually came a time of famine. Then First Mother, who had said, "My strength shall be felt all over the Earth," asked to be killed and buried. From her flesh grew the first wheat.

Mold for making the casting of Venus (right)

WILLENDORF VENUS
This stone Venus figurine from Willendorf, in Austria, represents a goddess and dates from the neolithic period (c. 5,000 B.C.). The exaggerated curves in this statue of the great mother goddess stress women's role in human fertility.

VENUS AND APHRODITE
Venus, the Roman goddess of love, beauty, and fertility, seems to have originally been a goddess of farmland and gardens before being identified with the Greek goddess Aphrodite. Aphrodite was concerned only with love; marriage was the reponsibility of Hera, and childbirth of her daughter Ilithyia.

Children of the gods

Matsya, the fish

IN MANY MYTHOLOGIES, THE GODS reproduce just as human beings do. Their children may be other gods (who may even take over from them), or semidivine heroes, such as Cuchulain and Hercules. Some supreme deities, such as the Norse god Odin and the Greek god Zeus, are called "all-father" in recognition of the role they play for other beings. However, not all children of the gods are beneficial to the world. For instance, the Norse god Loki gave birth to the fierce wolf Fenrir and Hel, the mistress of the underworld; the Greek god of the sea, Poseidon, fathered the brutal Cyclops Polyphemus. Gods can also incarnate themselves in human or animal form, as the Hindu god Vishnu does in his various guises, such as Narasimba, the half-man, half-lion; and Vamana, the dwarf.

Kurma, the turtle

INCARNATIONS OF VISHNU
The Hindu god Vishnu, the preserver, has been incarnated nine times in different forms. As the fish, Vishnu saved Manu, the first man, from the great flood. As the turtle, he helped the gods churn the ocean and win the elixir of immortality. Vishnu raised the Earth out of the sea as Varaha the boar. And as the hero Rama, he rescued his wife from a demon. Vishnu's tenth avatar, Kalki, the horse, will come to destroy and re-create the world at the end of this cycle of time.

Varaha, the boar

Cuchulain rides his chariot into battle

FATHER OF THE PHARAOHS
Falcon-headed Horus, whose eyes were the sun and the moon, was the child of the Egyptian gods Isis and Osiris. He was conceived when Isis breathed life into the mummified Osiris, who had been murdered by his brother Seth. The long battle between Horus and Seth was vicious, but eventually Horus prevailed. The Egyptian pharaohs traced their descent from him and were called the "living Horus."

UGLY WARRIOR
Cuchulain, a hero of Irish mythology, was a fierce warrior. His father was the sun god Lugh. Although normally very handsome, on the battlefield Cuchulain became a monster. One eye disappeared into his head, the other bulged; his heels turned to the front; and his jaws opened wide enough to swallow an enemy's head. Before he was killed, Cuchulain strapped himself to a standing stone so that he would die standing up.

Prince Rama

THE WATER TWINS
The Dogon people of Mali in West Africa say that the creator spirit Amma first mated with the Earth, and the Nommo (water) twins were born. Human on the top half and snakelike on the bottom half, the twins were made out of the life-force of Amma. The Nommo were green in color, and clothed their mother Earth with plants and trees. They are believed to make an outline of every newborn soul, giving it a twin nature, both male and female.

The Nommo stand between Earth and sky with their arms outstretched on this Dogon leader's stool

HEROIC HERACLES
The Greek hero Heracles (Hercules in Latin) was the son of Zeus by a mortal woman, Alcmene. As an infant he proved his divine descent by strangling two deadly serpents sent by Zeus's jealous wife Hera. Hera's hatred pursued Heracles all his life, robbing him of his destined throne.

Scary monsters

Giants are found throughout mythology. Their size makes them terrifying, but often they are portrayed as slow, stupid, and easily outwitted, like the Cyclops Polyphemus, who believes that the hero Odysseus's name is Nobody and yells out "Nobody is hurting me" when Odysseus blinds him. Many of the first beings were monsters, such as Ymir, the Norse frost giant.

Cyclopes had only one eye

Fierce incisors tear meat from the bone

ONE-EYED OGRE
Polyphemus was one of the legendary Cyclopes, one-eyed giants with ferocious appetites. He was blinded by Odysseus, who plunged a red-hot stake into his eye. But Polyphemus's father, Poseidon, was so enraged that he persecuted Odysseus — wrecking his ships, drowning his crews, and keeping him from his home for ten long years.

Skulls of mastodons (extinct elephant-like mammals) were once believed to be Cyclopes' skulls

Greedy Cyclopes could devour whole carcasses at one sitting

Tunic made from the hides of the Cyclops's prey

Cyclopes tore their prey limb from limb

Ancestor worship

IN MANY CULTURES, FEAR OF THE EVIL POWER of spirits of the dead is balanced by a belief in the protective power of the spirits of ancestors, who are believed to watch over and guide the living. For this reason offerings may be made to ancestors' shrines. For instance, in China the head of a family must make regular sacrifices of food at the graves of his ancestors; if not, the "hungry ghosts" may cause trouble. In both China and Japan, wooden tablets inscribed with the names of ancestors are kept in a household shrine. The duty that the living owe to the dead was never more pressing than in ancient Egypt, where it was vital that the eldest living son of deceased parents raise a monument to their memory and pronounce their names every time he passed it, to keep their names alive.

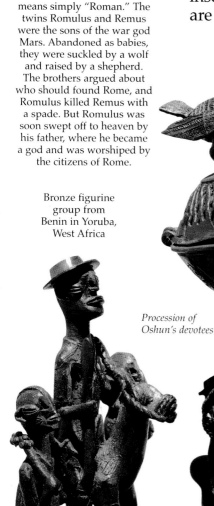

ROMULUS AND REMUS
Romulus was the mythical founder of Rome; his name means simply "Roman." The twins Romulus and Remus were the sons of the war god Mars. Abandoned as babies, they were suckled by a wolf and raised by a shepherd. The brothers argued about who should found Rome, and Romulus killed Remus with a spade. But Romulus was soon swept off to heaven by his father, where he became a god and was worshiped by the citizens of Rome.

Bronze figurine group from Benin in Yoruba, West Africa

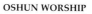
Procession of Oshun's devotees

OSHUN WORSHIP
Ancestors are worshiped in many parts of Africa and are prayed to for good health, fertility, and good fortune. The Yoruba people of West Africa worship Oshun, goddess of the river that bears the same name. Oshun was married to the thunder god Shango and has human descendants. People bathe in the Oshun River to protect themselves from disease. Women, in particular, consult the goddess Oshun in cases of family problems or illness.

Female figure from Middle Sepik River, Papua New Guinea

LIFE-GIVING ANCESTORS
In New Guinea, carved figures of ancestors were present at *moguru* (life-giving ceremonies) at which the young were initiated into adulthood and the men gained prowess as fighters. In the Papuan Gulf, the fierce Kerua headhunters hung human skulls from carved boards as offerings to ancestral beings.

COLOSSAL CHIEFS
On Easter Island, a remote and barren island of volcanic rock stranded in the eastern Pacific, stand hundreds of monolithic stone figures. They are *moai* — figures of dead chiefs who were regarded as descendants of the gods.

FEAST OF LANTERNS
The *bon* festival, held in Japan each July, is known as the Feast of Lanterns. It is held in honor of the spirits of the dead, which return to Earth for the three days of the festival. Relatives of the deceased pray at shrines, where they leave food and other treats for the spirits to feast on.

DREAMTIME ANCESTORS
The Dreamtime is the eternal present in which the revered ancestors of the Australian Aborigines exist, constantly creating the world. Creation story designs, shown to the Aborigines by the ancestors, are still painted on bodies, rocks, and bark, as in the painting (left) from Arnhem Land, North Australia. Aborigines carve pictures showing events in the Dreamtime on sacred wooden and stone artifacts, called *churinga*. These objects embody ancestral spiritual power and must not be seen by women or the uninitiated.

Papuan ancestral tablets, or ceremonial boards

Aboriginal stone knife similar to those used by the eternal ancestors to create humans

Bark sheath

Gap-toothed Louhi as an eagle-woman with scythe-like claws

Evil forces

Besides gods of death and sterility, there are many demons and forces of evil in world mythology. Balanced against these are forces of good which came into being to rid the world of evil. In Siberia it is told how the creator Ulgan made himself a companion, Erlik, from mud floating on the primal ocean. But Erlik, jealous of Ulgan, saved mud to try to build his own world, and he breathed life into humankind without Ulgan's permission. For these betrayals, Erlik was banished to the underworld, where he sits surrounded by evil spirits. Evil beings are very active in Hindu mythology, which has many antigods and demons. One of the most fearsome of all evil spirits is Vucub-Caquix, the Mayan monster macaw who claimed to be both the sun and the moon. He was killed in a terrible battle by the hero twins Hunahpu and Xbalanque, though not before he had torn off Hunahpu's arm.

WICKED LOUHI
The Finnish hag Louhi promised the smith Ilmarinen her daughter in return for the Sampo — a magic mill that grinds out grain, salt, and money. But Louhi proved treacherous, so Ilmarinen stole back the Sampo and set sail. Louhi turned into a bird and attacked the boat. In the struggle, the Sampo fell to the bottom of the sea, where it still grinds out salt to this day.

TREACHEROUS TRICKSTER
Loki, the Norse trickster god, turned against the other gods and brought about the death of Balder the Beautiful, son of the god Odin. For this, he is bound in agony, with poison dripping onto his face, until the final battle of Ragnarok, when he will lead an army from Hel against the gods in a ship made from dead men's nails.

CANNIBAL WITCH
Baba Yaga is the cannibal witch of Russian myth. She lives in a revolving hut supported by hen's feet, and travels through the air in a mortar. Her male equivalent is Koshchei the Deathless, who abducts maidens and can turn into a dragon.

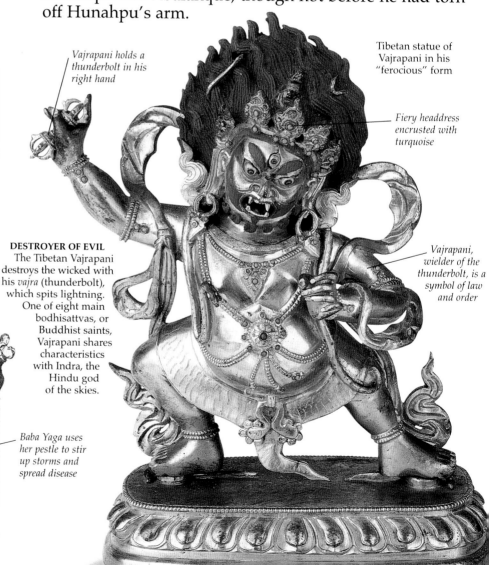

Vajrapani holds a thunderbolt in his right hand

Tibetan statue of Vajrapani in his "ferocious" form

Fiery headdress encrusted with turquoise

DESTROYER OF EVIL
The Tibetan Vajrapani destroys the wicked with his *vajra* (thunderbolt), which spits lightning. One of eight main bodhisattvas, or Buddhist saints, Vajrapani shares characteristics with Indra, the Hindu god of the skies.

Vajrapani, wielder of the thunderbolt, is a symbol of law and order

Baba Yaga uses her pestle to stir up storms and spread disease

SULKY SUSANO
While bathing, the Japanese god Izanagi gave birth to three powerful divinities: the sun goddess Amaterasu, moon god Tsuki-Yomi, and Susano, the god of storms and chaos. Susano was meant to rule the sea, but he threw a tantrum and said he would rather go to the underworld. He flung a skinned horse into Amaterasu's sacred weaving hall, so was banished to Earth. There he rescued Kusa-nada-hime, the Rice Paddy Princess, from an eight-headed dragon, and made her his wife.

Text from a 19th-century print of the storm god Susano and his wife

Rice Paddy Princess Kusa-nada-hime

FIRST HUMAN SACRIFICE
When the Aztec goddess Coatlicue was pregnant with the supreme god Huitzilopochtli, she was attacked and murdered by her jealous daughter, Coyolxauhqui, and Coyolxauhqui's 400 brothers. But Huitzilopochtli leaped fully formed from his mother's decapitated body and slew his sister, making her the first human sacrifice.

Each of Durga's ten hands holds a special weapon — a symbol of divine power

INVINCIBLE DURGA
The Hindu warrior goddess Durga was one of the guises of the great goddess Devi. Durga was created to fight the *asuras* (demon enemies of the gods), who had conquered heaven. In each of her ten hands Durga holds a special weapon that she used to cut off the head of the buffalo-king of the *asuras*.

Susano, the Japanese storm god

33

Superheroes

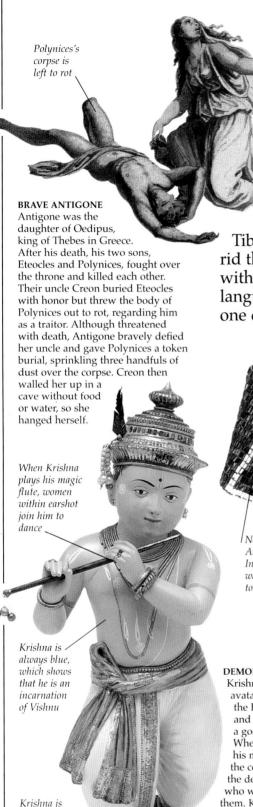

BRAVE ANTIGONE
Antigone was the daughter of Oedipus, king of Thebes in Greece. After his death, his two sons, Eteocles and Polynices, fought over the throne and killed each other. Their uncle Creon buried Eteocles with honor but threw the body of Polynices out to rot, regarding him as a traitor. Although threatened with death, Antigone bravely defied her uncle and gave Polynices a token burial, sprinkling three handfuls of dust over the corpse. Creon then walled her up in a cave without food or water, so she hanged herself.

Polynices's corpse is left to rot

MEN AND WOMEN WHO PERFORM great feats of daring and courage are celebrated in all mythologies. Often, they are said to be the children of gods or to be specially favored by the gods. Some heroes can defeat a whole series of enemies in single combat and rid countries of the monsters that plague them. Others, such as Hiawatha, are celebrated as peacemakers rather than as warriors. A typical hero is the Tibetan Gesar, who was a god chosen to be born as a man to rid the world of demons. Gesar became a powerful warrior king, with an immortal horse that flew through the sky and spoke all languages. At the end of his life, Gesar retired to heaven, but one day he will return, for evil can never be wholly defeated.

When Krishna plays his magic flute, women within earshot join him to dance

Krishna is always blue, which shows that he is an incarnation of Vishnu

Krishna is supported by a bed of lotus flowers

North American Indians made wampum (bead) belts to mark peace agreements

Beads are made from white and purple clam shells

DEMON DODGER
Krishna is the eighth avatar (incarnation) of the Hindu god Vishnu and is worshiped as a god in his own right. When he was a child, his mother took him to the countryside to escape the demon king Kansa, who was persecuting them. Kansa sent a female demon to poison him, but Krishna sucked the life out of her instead.

Sigurd kills the dragon

PEACEMAKER
Dekanah-wida was born to bring tidings of peace from the chief of the Sky Spirits to five warring Native American Indian tribes. Dekanah-wida made the Mohawk chief, Hiawatha, his peacemaker. Hiawatha then traveled between the tribes, persuading them to form the Iroquois League, whose members swore to live in peace together.

Fafnir the dragon

DRAGON SLAYER
The Scandinavian hero Sigurd slew the dragon Fafnir so that he could claim its treasure. Sigurd had been urged to kill the dragon by Regin, Fafnir's brother, who asked Sigurd to return with the dragon's heart. But Regin was plotting to kill Sigurd and steal the treasure for himself. Some birds tried to warn Sigurd, but he could not understand them. Fortunately as he cooked the dragon's heart he burned his thumb and putting it in his mouth, tasted the dragon's blood. The blood enabled Sigurd to understand the birds. Learning that Regin meant to betray him, Sigurd killed him and kept the treasure.

When Yi shot the suns, they fell to the Earth in the shape of crows

The Minotaur had a bull's head on a man's body

MONSTER KILLER

Theseus was the greatest of all Athenian heroes, said to be the son of the sea god Poseidon. His most famous feat was to slay the ferocious Minotaur. King Minos of Crete regularly fed the Minotaur with children from Athens; Theseus volunteered himself to be fed to the Minotaur and, with the help of Minos's daughter Ariadne, killed the Minotaur in the labyrinth (maze) in which he lived.

Yi won a potion of immortality, but Chang E drank it herself and floated to the moon

Heavenly gates are guarded by two soldiers

Mortals on their way to heaven to become immortals

Kneeling men and women mourn for the dead

Altars full of food

Scenes of the afterlife

YI THE ARCHER

The Chinese say that originally there were ten suns, the sons of the emperor of the eastern heavens. The suns took turns lighting the sky. But once, all ten went out to play. Together they were so hot that they began to scorch the Earth, so the emperor sent Yi, the heavenly archer, to teach them a lesson. Yi shot down nine of them. The emperor was so upset that he stripped Yi and his wife, Chang E, of their immortality and banished them from heaven.

Perseus holds Medusa's severed head

GREEK GUARDIAN

Perseus was the son of the Greek god Zeus and the maiden Danaë. To save his mother from an unwanted marriage, Perseus agreed to fetch the head of the Gorgon Medusa, whose glance turned the onlooker to stone. Using a bronze shield as a mirror so that he did not have to meet the Gorgon's gaze, Perseus cut off her head. He then used the head to turn his mother's unwelcome suitor to stone.

Gilgamesh clutches a captured lion cub

KING GILGAMESH

Gilgamesh was the great hero of ancient Mesopotamia. He was a semidivine king, who fought monsters with his friend Enkidu. When Gilgamesh scorned the love of the goddess Ishtar, she sent a great bull to destroy him, but Gilgamesh and Enkidu slew the bull.

Chinese funeral banner, 2nd century B.C.

Medusa lies dead at Perseus's feet

Divine weapons

Sᴡᴏʀᴅ, sᴘᴇᴀʀ, ᴀx, ᴀɴᴅ ʙᴏᴡ — the weapons of the gods often mirror those of humans. The Norse all-father Odin, for instance, had a magical spear that he used to stir up war. But the gods can also unleash natural forces as weapons, most notably the thunderbolt (lightning), which has been a weapon of sky gods all over the world. Weapons could be improvised out of anything: the club of the semidivine Greek hero Heracles was simply an uprooted olive tree. The Navajo hero twins were given bows with arrows of lightning by their father, the sun god, to help them rid the world of monsters. Even when caught without their weapons, gods can punish the insolent or wicked. When the Greek hunter Actaeon spied the goddess Diana bathing, without her bow and arrows, she turned him into a stag and let his own hounds maul him to death.

The Greek god Zeus wields a thunderbolt

BATTLING BROTHERS
This 19th-century chief's ax is a symbol of Tane, the Oceanic god of the forests, who was himself shaped by craftsmen with axes. After Tane separated Earth and sky, he and his brother Tangaroa, god of the seas, began a fierce battle. Tangaroa lashed the land with his waves, trying to wash it away. Tane supplied men with canoes, spears, fishhooks, and nets to catch Tangaroa's fish. Craftsmen pray to Tane to put their axes to sleep at night, and to wake them up in the morning.

Shango looks both ways, so that no one can escape him

THUNDER AND LIGHTNING
The terrifying energy of an electrical storm has been interpreted by many people as the anger of the gods. Thunderbolts have been used as weapons by many gods, including the Olympian Zeus. Native Americans revere the Thunderbird, which produces thunder by flapping its wings and lightning by flashing its eyes. Tupan, an Amazonian thunder god, caused thunder and lightning by crossing the sky in a wooden trough.

SPITTER OF THUNDERBOLTS
Ceremonial staffs such as this symbolize Shango, thunder god of the Yoruba people of West Africa. His symbol is the double ax, which represents thunderbolts. Shango was originally a king and was given the power to spit thunderbolts by the trickster god Eshu. Being hit by lightning is thought to be a sign of Shango's anger.

To terrify Shango's enemies, his devotees hold thunderbolt staffs as they dance to loud drumbeats

MAGICAL SWORD
The Norse god Frey had a sword that would fight on its own. But he gave the sword to Skirnir, his servant, as a reward for winning him the hand of the beautiful maiden Gerd. It is said that at the final battle of Ragnarok, Frey will fight the fire giant Surt, who has a blade that flames like the sun. But without his sword, Frey will be defeated, allowing Surt to burn up the world.

Iron sword from Denmark

ANCESTRAL WEAPON
The boomerang was an important weapon of the Australian Aborigines. The first boomerang represented the Aboriginal Rainbow Snake, and is said to have been made from the tree between heaven and Earth. A myth of the Binbinga tribe of Australia tells how the ancestral snake Bobbi-Bobbi made the first boomerang from one of his ribs.

Rainbow Snake

Aboriginal war boomerangs are designed to fly in straight lines and travel great distances

17th-century brass *vajras* from Tibet representing thunderbolts

BLADE OF IRON
Ogun is the god of iron and war among the Yoruba people of West Africa. When the Earth was still a watery waste, Ogun used to climb down from heaven on a spider's web to hunt in the marshland. After the Earth was formed, Ogun cleared the land with his iron blade. He was last seen sinking into the ground with his sword.

Ritual sword used in Ogun worship

Ceremonial bow and arrows

GODDESS OF HUNTING
Diana is the Roman name for the Greek goddess of hunting and archery, Artemis. Although Diana was the goddess of the hunt, she was also the protector of all wild animals.

Vows taken in the name of Ogun, with the tongue on a blade or some other iron object, are completely binding

Diana, protector of wild animals

Silver replica of Thor's hammer from Denmark

Tibetans use vajras, *believed to hold magical powers, in rituals and while meditating*

Thor in his chariot pulled by goats

THOR'S LUCKY HAMMER
The Norse thunder god Thor was the son of the all-father Odin; his mother was the Earth. He had a wonderful hammer, *Mjollnir*, which never missed its target, and returned to his hand when thrown. Vikings wore pendants in the shape of Thor's hammer for protection. Large replicas of these lucky hammers were also used to bless weddings, births, and funerals.

Gods of war

HUMAN HISTORY HAS BEEN SHAPED by war and conflict, and gods of war have a high status in many mythologies. The Greeks had two war gods: Ares, who was the god of fighting; and Athena, who was the goddess of strategy. That a goddess should take an interest in warfare is not unusual. Ishtar was the Mesopotamian goddess of both love and war; the Irish had a triple war goddess, the Morrigan, who could change into a crow and settled in that form on the shoulder of the dying hero Cuchulain. But most war gods are male, and many of them, like Ares and Odin, are bloodthirsty, reveling in slaughter.

GREEK GODDESS OF STRATEGY
While Ares was the Greek god of fighting, Athena was the goddess of strategy and wisdom. She sprang from the head of her father Zeus, fully armed and ready for battle. Athena is always depicted in full armor, with the head of the Gorgon Medusa fixed to her breastplate.

The divine blacksmith Gu taught the first humans how to make tools so that they could work the land

Mars wears a warrior's helmet

PROTECTIVE MARS
Mars was the Roman god of war. He seems to have been originally a god of agriculture, and even as a war god he retained a protective function, unlike his brutal and violent Greek equivalent, Ares. He was one of the most important Roman gods and was believed to have fathered Romulus, the founder of Rome. Soldiers made sacrifices to Mars before and after battle.

GOD OF IRON
Gu was the fifth-born child of Mawu-Lisa, the West African creator god. Mawu gave her strength to Gu. He is made of iron and is sometimes depicted as an iron sword. In this form, Mawu-Lisa used him to clear the Earth for humans to live in. Gu is the god of iron and consequently of war, since war is waged with iron weapons.

Iron statue of Gu, war god of the Fon people of West Africa

WARRING KU
Ku was the war god of Hawaii. He had many names descriptive of his various roles. As patron of woodworkers he was Ku-adzing-out-the-canoe. When the gods were trapped between their parents Earth and sky, Ku-of-the-angry-face wanted to kill them, but the other gods fought Ku. This was the beginning of warfare.

Valkyries rode horses to fetch dead warriors from the battlefield and take them to Odin's Valhalla

FIGHTING SPIRITS
The Valkyries of the Norse god Odin were female spirits who rode to battle to give victory or death, according to Odin's will. They also waited on the souls of dead warriors in the hall of Valhalla. The name Valkyrie means "chooser of the slain." The Norse fertility goddess Freya was said to ride to battle and claim half the slain.

All-father Odin wears an elaborate winged helmet

Chinese bronze sword, 4th century B.C.

NORSE WAR GODS
The Viking gods were among the most warlike of all. Their leader, Odin (left), was the god of battle, inspiring his warriors with a fighting frenzy. Only those who died in battle joined him in Valhalla after death.

Spears were among Norse warriors' most prized possessions

DEMON KILLER
Skanda, the six-headed Hindu god of war, is the son of Shiva. He was born to kill the demon Taraka, who had been oppressing the gods. Skanda rides a peacock, on which he traveled around the world in a contest of learning with his brother Ganesh. Ganesh, who stayed at home and read, knew more than Skanda when he returned.

CHINESE WARRIOR GOD
Guan Di is the Chinese god of war. Originally a humble seller of bean curd, he devoted himself to study, and he is still regarded as a patron of literature. However, after he killed a magistrate, he had to flee his home and fend for himself. Guan Di became a soldier, one of the three famous Brothers of the Peach Orchard, and, in 1594 A.D., was elevated to the status of god of war.

Statue of Guan Di, the Chinese god of war

Contacting the spirits

ANCIENT GREEKS TOOK THEIR PROBLEMS to the oracle of Apollo at Delphi, where a priestess, called the pythoness, went into a trance and uttered strange words that were then interpreted by a priest. Among the Vikings, *volvas* (prophetesses), answered questions in a similar way. Siberian shamans, Native American medicine men, and Aboriginal men of high degree all use drumming, dance, and song to enter an altered mental state in which they can communicate with the spirit world. Offerings and sacrifices may also bridge the gap between the two worlds, as when worshipers are possessed by the gods in voodoo rites. Among the Yoruba of West Africa, the god of fate, Eshu, uses sacrifices to plead with the other gods, or to appease evil spirits on behalf of humanity.

GUIDING GOD
The Greek god Hermes (Mercury in Rome) was the messenger of the gods, and also the guide of souls into the underworld. As he was always going to and fro, he became the protector of all travelers.

Pipe of carved human bone

Priest speaks into this hole to distort his voice and make it boom out

VOICE DISGUISER
A priest of the Tiv people of Nigeria would use this voice disguiser to allow the ancestor god Tiv to speak through him in a piercing cry.

Half-halo represents Ganesh's divinity

Noose to trap delusion

CONVEYOR OF PRAYERS
Ganesh, the wise elephant-headed son of Shiva, is the god of all good enterprises. Hindus ask Ganesh to pass on their requests to Shiva. They make offerings to the potbellied god before going on a journey, starting a business, or making plans for a wedding.

豊川閣霊槙守護攸

Jizo, the protector of children and travelers

GOOD-LUCK CHARMS
Japanese *fuda*, or amulets, bear the name of a god and are used to ward off evil and misfortune and to bring good luck. They are often placed on household shrines to protect the family.

The ancestors sit in the top branches of the world tree; the shaman climbs up to ask for their help

Shamans' spirit helpers often take animal form

Drumbeats are used to call the spirits that will help the shaman

Metal ornaments hanging from the belt protect against evil spirits

THE SHAMAN
A shaman is someone who has had a life-changing vision that enables him or her to enter a trance and fly to the spirit world. A shaman's power is usually used for healing, though it can also cause disease or death.

Souls of the unborn nest in the tree

Dancers hang from rawhide thongs sewn through the skin

SUN DANCE
In rituals such as the sun dance, Plains Native Americans underwent excruciating physical tortures as sacrifices to the Great Spirit. Once they had fulfilled their vows, dancers hoped to receive a vision.

The pipe bowl is round, like the world, and outside it is the endless universe

38457

PIPES OF PEACE
The sacred pipe is an important part of many Native American rituals, bringing peace and healing. Tobacco was believed to have the power to summon good spirits, ward off evil ones, and bring either good luck or bad. Communal smoking helped to reinforce the ties between families, tribes, and the universe.

Tiger spirits often teach shamans their craft

The world tree houses all souls

Spirits

Siberian shaman's outfit

Love, fortune, and happiness

MANY PEOPLE WORSHIP deities who will bring them luck in life. In ancient times, for instance, the Romans had a cult of the goddess Fortuna (good luck). The Ewe people of Togo in West Africa believe that the soul of each unborn child must first visit Ngolimeno, the "Mother of the Spirit People." If they please her, she will grant them a happy life. The Japanese worship seven gods of luck, of whom one, Benten, is a goddess. But it is the Chinese who have outdone all others in the worship of fortune and happiness. The lucky Ho-Ho twins (right) are often shown attending Tsai Shen, the god of wealth. Another common trio is Fu Shen, god of happiness; Lu Shen, god of good luck; and Shou Shen, god of longevity.

THE WINGED GOD
Cupid (Eros in Greek) was the mischievous Roman god of love, often shown as a cheeky infant with a bow and arrows. Some of his arrows had gold tips and caused people to fall in love; others were tipped with lead and had the opposite effect.

Venus of Rome rises from the ocean on a scallop shell

BORN OF FOAM
The Greek goddess of love and desire, Aphrodite (Venus to the Romans), was born from the foam of the sea. She devoted herself to pleasure, prided herself on never doing any work, and was often assisted by Eros (Cupid to the Romans). Aphrodite was married to the smith god Hephaestus but had many lovers among both gods and men. As Venus she was the mother of the Roman hero Aeneas.

Each twin carries a jar containing a lotus of purity and perfection

Statue depicting the birth of Aphrodite, Greek goddess of love

Terracotta figure of Aphrodite made in the 2nd century B.C

The gods are standing on beds of lotus flowers

The head of each twin is decorated with a lotus

These Ho-Ho gods symbolize happy relations between couples

GOOD FORTUNE GODS
The seven gods of luck (Shichi Fukujin) include Bishamon, Daikoku, Ebisu, Fukurokuju, Hotei, Jorojin, and the goddess Benten – the bringer of love, happiness, and good fortune. The Shichi Fukujin are often shown together on their treasure ship. Their treasures include a hat of invisibility, a lucky rain hat, keys to the divine treasure house, a purse that never empties, a cloak of feathers, rolls of silk, and scrolls or books.

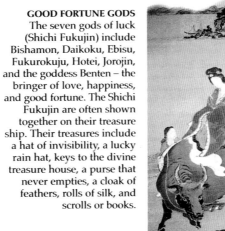

Benten rides an ox, symbol of good fortune

CONFUSED DEITY
Kwan-non is the god or goddess of mercy in Japanese Buddhism. Priests regard Kwan-non as a male divinity, but most people pray to him as a goddess, and he appears in 33 female forms. This statue shows her (or him) holding a baby. Expectant mothers would pray to this statue as Koyasu Kwan-non ("Kwan-non of easy childbirth").

Love medicines are inserted into pockets on the chest of each doll

LOVE DOLLS
These Native American medicine dolls are used by the Menominee of the western Great Lakes to ensure that a husband and wife remain faithful to each other. The male doll is named after the husband and the female after the wife, and the two are tied together face to face. The Pottawatomi, also of the western Great Lakes, used dolls as charms to make one person fall in love with another.

HO-HO TWINS
The two immortals called Ho are the patrons of Chinese merchants. Besides bringing prosperity, they represent harmonious union between couples, because the word "ho" means harmony. Their names were originally Han Shan and Shih-teh. Han Shan was a holy fool who attached himself to the monastery at Kuo-ching Ssu; the monks rejected him, but Shih-teh, an orphan in the kitchens, saved scraps to feed him.

Tricksters

LIGHTHEARTED COMEDY and dark humor are introduced into myths by trickster figures, such as the Native American Coyote (left), whose insatiable curiosity and love of mischief leave havoc and confusion in their wake. Tricksters may be animal, human, or both. Some tricksters hover between good and evil, as does the cunning Norse god Loki. The Ashanti people of West Africa tell tales of Anansi, the cunning spider-man, who won the famous stories of the sky god Nyame. By a series of clever tricks, Anansi trapped all the creatures that Nyame thought were impossible to catch. For instance, he caught the fairy Mmoatia by making a tar baby, to which Mmoatia stuck fast. When Anansi delivered the creatures to Nyame, he was so impressed that he willingly gave Anansi the stories. Since then, the tales have been called spider stories.

WILY COYOTE
Many Native American peoples tell stories of the wily Coyote, who both tricks and is tricked. Coyote has many human characteristics — he is greedy and selfish, and his exploits lead to bad as well as good consequences.

Cowrie shells are used by Eshu to predict the future

MISCHIEVOUS ESHU
Eshu is the trickster god of the Yoruba people of West Africa. His many guises include giant, dwarf, rude boy, wise old man, and a priest, as seen here. Eshu loves mischief. For instance, he broke up a firm friendship between two men by wearing a hat that was white on one side but black on the other, causing them to quarrel about the color of his hat.

Eshu holds a small statue of himself

Hare climbs up the mask

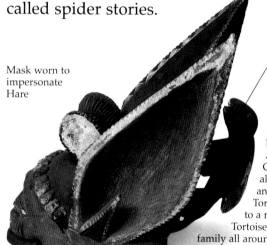

Mask worn to impersonate Hare

CUNNING HARE
Hare is an African animal trickster who became known in America as Brer Rabbit. Cunning and wily, Hare always outwits the other animals, except when Tortoise challenged him to a race. Instead of running, Tortoise placed members of his family all around the course and sat waiting for Hare at the finish line.

Figures represent Eshu in his various guises

An Eshu priest would wear this statue by hooking the headdress over his shoulder, just as Eshu is doing with the statue he is holding

Medicine calabashes (bowls) represent Eshu's magical powers

SUN CATCHER
Maui-of-a-thousand-tricks is the trickster hero of Polynesian mythology. He fished up the islands with his magic hook, pushed up the heavens, stole fire for humankind, and snared the sun with his sister's hair to slow it down, so that we have long summer days.

Tengu rescue the hero Tametomo from the jaws of a giant fish

INVISIBLE TRICKSTERS
The Tengu are Japanese trickster spirits, part-bird, part-man. They are said to be descended from the storm god Susano, who himself got into trouble by playing tricks. Tengu have magic cloaks of invisibility.

The fish represents the islands that Maui fished up from the sea

GRIMACING GOD
Bes was a popular Egyptian god of music, dance, and laughter, whose grimacing face and comical antics were thought to frighten away evil spirits. He was the protector of mothers in childbirth and the companion of young children. He is always shown sticking his tongue out at the world.

Bacchus's long flowing hair shows his eternal youth

INDULGENT GOD
Bacchus (Dionysus in Greek) was the Roman god of wine and ecstasy. His followers were wild women called the Maenads (frenzied ones). When sailors captured Bacchus, his tricks sent them diving madly into the sea, where they turned into dolphins. It was Bacchus who gave King Midas the double-edged gift of turning all that he touched into gold.

Animal idols

Gods and spirits may be shown in animal form, or as half-human, half-beast. Trickster figures, such as the African spider-man Anansi, may be a man, an animal, or a mixture of both at different times in the same story. Some gods have an animal helper, such as the fox that lived with the Japanese rice god Inari and acted as his messenger. Some gods can transform themselves into animals; the Greek god Zeus, for example, became a bull and then a swan while pursuing his love affairs. Some gods have an animal double, as with the Aztec god Quetzalcoatl and his twin Xolotl — the dog who helped retrieve the bones of humankind from the underworld.

Celtic drinking horns tipped with sheeps' heads

THE HORNED ONE
Gods with animals' horns are found in many mythologies. One of the most famous was the Celtic horned god Cernunnos, who was lord of the beasts, and a god of fertility. The goat's horns of the Greek god Pan inspired pictures of the Christian Devil.

THE BULL OF HEAVEN
This winged bull stood guard over a royal palace in Assyria. The bull was a cult animal all over ancient west Asia. For instance, a bull of heaven was sent to destroy the Sumerian hero Gilgamesh. But Gilgamesh and his friend slew the bull and gave its heart to the sun god Shamash.

Half-human, half-beast

The gods of many peoples are often depicted as half-human, half-animal. This is especially true of the Egyptian gods, nearly all of whom have at least one animal form. For instance, the cow goddess Hathor was also worshipped as the lioness Sekhmet, and the cat Bastet. The dog or jackal god Anubis could also become a snake or a falcon. The sun god Ra turned himself into a cat to cut off the head of the evil snake Apep that attacked him every night.

Nagas have both protective and destructive powers

19th-century Sri Lankan mask

Fierce face wards off the evil spirits thought to cause sickness

THE SNAKE DEMON
This mask of Naga Rassa, or snake demon, is worn in dances to drive away evil spirits. The nagas (sacred snakes) were descended from the ancient sage Kasyapa, the father of life. Buddhists tell how Mucilinda, a king of the nagas, grew more heads to shelter the Buddha from a storm.

SEKHMET
The sun god Ra sent the raging lioness Sekhmet to destroy humankind. But when Ra changed his mind, the only way to stop Sekhmet from killing was to make her drunk.

SOBEK
The Egyptian crocodile-god Sobek was unable to resist eating meat, so when the dismembered body of the god Osiris was thrown into the Nile, Sobek gulped some of it down. He was punished for this crime by having his tongue cut out.

ANUBIS
The jackal-headed god Anubis made the first mummy when he wrapped the body parts of the god Osiris in cloth to put them back together. In the underworld, Anubis weighed the hearts of the dead against the feather of justice.

46

When Garuda soars into the sky, he symbolizes the human spirit

Golden Garuda's body shines as bright as the sun — some say he was the sun in the form of a bird

Vishnu and his wife, Lakshmi, ride on Garuda

Eagle-like wings

Garuda has the body of a human

Legs are covered with golden feathers

KING OF THE BIRDS
Half-human, half-bird, Garuda was the Hindu king of the birds and destroyer of evil. He was ridden by the great god Vishnu. Garuda was the son of Kasyapa (left). But Garuda hated his father's other offspring, the nagas, because their mother made his mother, Vinata, a slave in the underworld. To save her, Garuda had to steal a cup of the elixir of immortality from the gods.

Clawed feet enabled Garuda to pick up the snakes that he devoured

Brass figure of Garuda from Tibet

Mythical beasts

STORIES ABOUT MYTHICAL CREATURES are found all over the world. Native Americans say that many monsters peopled the world at the beginning of time, until great heroes defeated them. Some people believe that mythical beasts are based on garbled accounts of real creatures — that unicorns, for instance, are really rhinoceroses. But mythical creatures seem to be more a focus for fear, awe, and wonder than simply mistaken natural history. Monsters are sometimes combinations of various animals, such as the griffin, which was half-eagle, half-lion. Just giving an ordinary animal a special feature, such as the ability of the Greek horse Pegasus to fly, transports it from the ordinary world to a realm of wonder.

WILD HORSES
Half-man, half-horse, the centaur was a wild and savage creature. One exception was Chiron, a wise centaur, who was tutor to many Greek heroes. He died after being accidentally wounded by Heracles with a poisoned arrow.

CREATURES OF THE DEEP
In the past, sailors returned from their travels with strange beasts, which they claimed to have fished from the sea. The creature "Jenny Haniver" (above) is actually a dried skate fish. Some of these curious creatures were created by joining the bodies of different animals together. For instance, a monkey's body was grafted onto the tail of a fish to create a merman.

Spiky claws protrude from the dragon's wings

BLOWING HOT AIR
Fire-breathing, winged dragons, who jealously guard their hoards of treasure, feature in many European myths. For instance, the Scandinavian dragon Fafnir was actually a man who turned into a dragon to protect his treasure. Many stories tell of dragon-slaying heroes who rescue maidens or win their hands in marriage. One such hero was Tristan, the Celtic hero who killed a dragon to win the hand of Isolde. Unlike the fearsome European dragon, Chinese dragons are kindly and serpentlike.

Dragons breathe fire through their mouths

Unicorn horns were prized for their supposed ability to detect poison

HORN OF PURITY
The unicorn was a white horselike creature, with a single spiral horn growing from its forehead. It was said that if a unicorn dipped its horn into water, the water would become pure. In fact, the unicorn was such a powerful symbol of purity that supposed unicorn horns (actually the tusks of narwhal whales) once sold for 20 times their weight in gold; one was even said to be worth a city.

DREADFUL LOCKS
Medusa was one of the three Gorgons — hideous creatures with snakes for hair. Anyone who looked at her would be turned to stone. But the Greek hero Perseus killed Medusa by looking at her reflection in a bronze shield as he cut off her head.

Medusa's hair was made of writhing snakes

WINGS OF A HERO
The winged horse Pegasus was ridden by the Greek hero Bellerophon. When his enemies ordered Bellerophon to kill the monstrous Chimera (below), they hoped he would die in the attempt. Instead, however, riding Pegasus, Bellerophon swooped down on the monster from above and riddled it with arrows.

Pegasus was born from Medusa's blood

A serpent formed the Chimera's tail

The middle part of the Chimera was a she-goat

European dragons have batlike wings

Thorny hooks protrude from the dragon's tail

HEADS AND TAILS
The Chimera was a fire-breathing monster made up of the body parts of various animals. It was one of the children of the half-nymph, half-serpent Echidna, who also spawned such monsters as the Sphinx and the 100-headed serpent Ladon. The Chimera was slain by the Greek hero Bellerophon.

The Chimera had the forequarters of a lion

The dragon's skin is covered in scales like those of a serpent or fish

Clawed feet are seen on both Chinese and European dragons

Painting the story

THERE ARE MANY WAYS OF TELLING stories other than through speech, and many myths are "told" through ritual, dance, or art rather than through narrative storytelling. In the chantways (right) of the Native American Navajo, sand painting, song, prayer, dance, and ritual combine to relive complex myths, which are remembered not for their story content but for their healing spiritual power. The Australian Aboriginal stories of the Dreamtime are recalled not just in words and ceremonies but also through traditional designs painted on the body. The same designs are used in bark paintings and the ground paintings of central Australia, which are very similar to Navajo sand paintings.

BEATING THE DRUM
Across Africa, drums are used to beat out rhythms to accompany reenactment rituals and dances. A drum is thought to have a spirit living in it, which may possess those who dance to its beat. The *bata* drum, used by the Yoruba tribe of West Africa in ceremonies to honor the thunder god Shango, is said to have been made by Shango to frighten his enemies.

The headdress varies in size and design, according to the character

Noble characters paint their faces green

Heroes wear red jackets

Ankle bracelets

Wooden snake stick (symbol of lightning)

SNAKE DANCE
Native Americans held rituals to ensure rain and good crops. In the Hopi snake dance, dancers hold live snakes in their mouths. Snake sticks are set up in ceremonial chambers. After the dance, the snakes are released to take the dancers' prayers to the gods.

STORIES THROUGH DANCE
Kathakali dancers enact stories from the two great epics of India, the Mahabharata and the Ramayana. The essence of both stories is the eternal struggle between good and evil, and dances usually end with the conquering of a demon by a hero.

Beats of the double-sided drum call up new creations

The skirt is made up of many layers of white cotton

RING OF FLAMES
The Hindu god Siva dances the tandava, which represents the creation and destruction of the world. He dances in a circle of flames — one hand cupping the flame of destruction, the other holding the drum of creation. As he dances, Siva tramples the dwarf of ignorance beneath his feet.

Mudstone

Sandstone

Gypsum

Sacred sandpainting

The sand paintings of the Native American Navajo are temporary altars created and destroyed as part of healing rituals known as chantways. Their Navajo name means "place where the gods come and go." Each painting must be re-created in exactly the same way each time, or the ritual will not work.

Chalk

Brown pigment

Yellow pigment

Red pigment

Charcoal

POWDER PAINTS
Sand painting pigments are gathered by the family sponsoring the ceremony and ground in a mortar and pestle. Pigments include sandstone, mudstone, charcoal from hard oak, cornmeal, powdered flower petals, and plant pollen.

CHANTWAY CEREMONIES
Sand paintings are made by skilled painters under the direction of the singer who is in charge of the ritual. An average sand painting takes six men about four hours to complete. When the painting is finished, the singer sprinkles it with protective pollen and says a prayer; then the ritual begins.

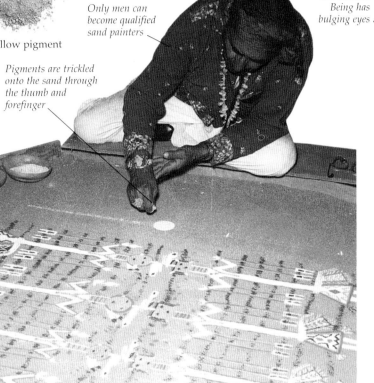

Only men can become qualified sand painters

Pigments are trickled onto the sand through the thumb and forefinger

The Oculate Being has bulging eyes

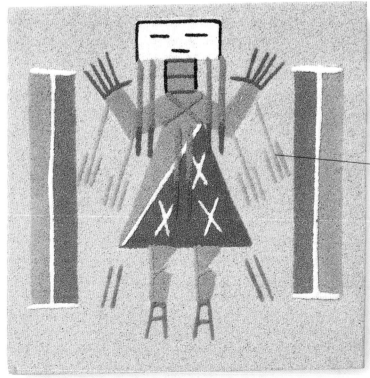

POWERFUL PICTURES
Sand paintings contain exact depictions of the Navajo " holy people" — supernatural beings whose powers are evoked in the chantway ceremonies. Such sand paintings are sacred and powerful. This nonsacred sand painting, made for commercial sale, shows a typical holy person.

Bracelets and armlets hang from the wrists and elbows

Snake-like tongue

WOVEN STORY
This woven textile from the Paracas people of Peru is full of the spirits and demons of Paracas mythology, including bug-eyed Oculate Beings, shown as heads with no bodies and long tongues snaking out between prominent teeth.

Alpaca wool weaving from southern Peru, 600–200 B.C.

TURTLE WORLD
Many Native
American peoples
believe that the Earth
is supported on the back of a turtle — a
belief that is also found in Hindu mythology.
The creator god Brahma took the shape of a
turtle to create the world. Vishnu became
a turtle to help the gods win the elixir of
immortality. In North America and in
Africa the turtle is also a trickster figure.

Universal creatures

MANY COMMON THEMES run through world
mythology. One theme connects human beings
with other animals — we are descended from them,
or they are our reincarnated ancestors, or they
represent gods or spirits whom we must worship or
appease. In many creation myths, such as the stories
of the Aboriginal Dreamtime, the first inhabitants
of the world are neither animal nor human but a
mixture of both. This is true of many "animal"
gods, such as the African spider-man Anansi. The
Egyptian gods all have one or more animal forms as
well as human forms; even in the Judeo-Christian
tradition the devil can take
the form of a snake.

*Eyes of
inlaid
turquoise*

Native
American
Anasazi
frog, symbol
of water

THE FROG
A West African story telling how Frog brought death
into the world is echoed by a Native American myth
which says that Frog was so angry with his Maker
that he spat poison into the Maker's water, killing
him and all his creatures. To the Maori of New
Zealand, the frog was a rain god, an association
also made by Native Americans. In Egypt Heket
was a frog goddess of childbirth and resurrection.

Recurring crocodiles

Because of their fearsome
appearance, crocodiles appear
in many myths. Often they are
threatening creatures — for instance
the Basuto tribe of Africa believes
that a crocodile can seize a man's
shadow and pull him under water.
But on the island of Sulawesi, in
Indonesia, crocodiles are addressed
as "grandfather" because they may
be an ancestor. And it is believed that a
crocodile will attack a human only when
told to do so by the god Poe Mpalaburu.

*Detail from a
Papuan shield*

*Man inside
the belly of
a crocodile*

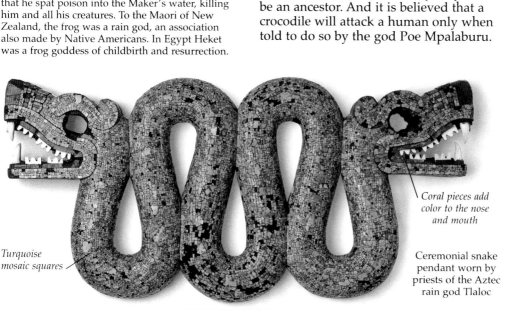

*Turquoise
mosaic squares*

*Coral pieces add
color to the nose
and mouth*

Ceremonial snake
pendant worn by
priests of the Aztec
rain god Tlaloc

LIFE-GIVING SERPENT
The snake is probably the most widely revered creature in world mythology. It is often
associated with the primal waters from which all life was created. In the Americas, the
double-headed serpent is associated with life-giving rain. Australian Aborigines credit
the creation of the landscape to the Rainbow Snake, the source of shamanic power. The
Rainbow Snake Aido-Hwedo arches over the sky and under the sea in West Africa.

FATHER CROCODILE
Papuans believe that crocodiles
have magical powers. One myth
of the Kiwai Papuans tells how
the creator, Ipila, carved the first
four humans from wood and
gave them sago to eat. But two
of them began to eat meat and
turned into crocodile-men. The
clans descended from them claim
the crocodile as their father.

Egyptian
crocodile god
Sobek

Mayan crocodile
incense burner

*The crocodile has
large, snapping jaws
with very sharp teeth*

HEAVENLY MONSTER
In Mayan art there are numerous depictions of
the celestial, or cosmic, monster, a being with a
crocodile's body and two heads, one at the front
and one at the back. The monster is sometimes
shown arching
over the heavens,
its body in the
form of clouds.

Clawed feet

*Golden crocodile
figure made by the
Ashanti people of
West Africa*

*Dry, scaly skin
prevents water
loss in the hot
African sun*

*Back feet
are webbed*

Nile crocodiles
are found on
riverbanks
throughout
tropical Africa

*Powerful,
whiplike tail*

AFRICAN ANCESTORS
Many Africans believe crocodiles
to be reincarnated people. In West
Africa it is said that a person who
kills a crocodile will become one.
And if someone is attacked by a
crocodile, it is believed that the
victim must have harmed the
crocodile during its human life.

RAVENOUS SOBEK
Ancient Egyptians worshipped
crocodiles in the form of the crocodile
god Sobek, who was often depicted with
the head of a crocodile and the body of a
human. Sobek was so hungry that when the
dismembered body of Osiris was thrown into
the Nile, he ate some of it. The other gods
cut out Sobek's tongue for this wicked act.

Death and the underworld

SINCE HUMANITY BEGAN, PEOPLE HAVE told stories to explain what happens after death. The Mayan hero twins Hunahpu and Xbalanque descended to Xibalba, the "place of fright," to rescue their father from One Death, lord of the underworld. The twins survived ordeals in the houses of lances, fire, and jaguars. They then boasted that they had power over death, and to prove it let themselves be killed and ground like flour. When they came back to life, the lords of death were so impressed that they asked to be killed too. But the twins did not revive them, and so the power of death was lessened forever. In his top hat and dark glasses, the Haitian voodoo god Ghede guards the eternal crossroads where the souls of the dead pass their way to the underworld.

The skeleton is commonly used as an image of death

CHINESE JUDGE OF THE DEAD
Yen-lo is the terrifying ruler and judge of the dead in China. First, the souls are weighed: the virtuous are light, the sinful heavy. Then the souls must pass a number of tests and challenges. They are assaulted by demons, attacked by dogs, then allowed one last glimpse of home and family before being given a drink that wipes away all memories. Finally, each soul is reincarnated.

DYING FOR DISOBEDIENCE
The elaborate funeral rites of the Dogon people of West Africa involve dancing and chanting in a secret language. These rituals recount a myth that describes how death entered the world because of the disobedience of young men. Africans do not see death as a final end but believe that the spirits of the dead have power over the living.

Osiris, god of the underworld

Horus, son of Osiris

THE AFTERLIFE
The ancient Egyptians believed that their souls would be weighed against the feather of truth, and that they would then be led into the Hall of the Two Truths to face the lord of the dead, Osiris. The virtuous hoped for a new life in the Field of Reeds, a perfected version of Egypt.

Skirts are red to represent death

AZTEC LORD OF THE UNDERWORLD

Mictlantecuhtli, the Aztec god of death, is usually depicted as a white skeleton spotted with blood. On their way to his peaceful underworld (Mictlan), the dead were reduced to skeletons by a wind of knives. Mictlantecuhtli was said to be the father of Quetzalcoatl, the lord of life.

The grinning Mictlantecuhtli welcomes the dead to his underworld

DAY OF THE DEAD

The Mexican Day of the Dead (November 1) is an occasion for great festivities. Every family prays to the souls of dead relatives so that they will return to Earth for one night. Altars in homes and cemeteries are decorated with food, flowers, and ghoulish sugar models. A candle is lit for each soul to help it find its way back to the land of the living. Many other cultures celebrate a day of the dead, including the Chinese, where it is known as the Feast of the Hungry Ghosts.

Altar skulls are made from sugar and water and are decorated with sugar icing

Souls of the dead are tormented by demons in hell

VISIONS OF HELL

Eternal torment in the underworld is the fate of sinners in many cultures. The Greeks in particular devised ingenious fates for those who offended the gods. Sisyphus (who told tales on Zeus) was forced to spend eternity rolling a stone uphill, only to see it roll back to the ground just as he was reaching the top. Tantalus (who served the gods his own son at a banquet) was condemned to stand neck-high in water, with ripe fruit dangling over his head, never able to eat or drink.

Norse chieftains were cremated in longboats to transport them to Valhalla

WARRIORS' HEAVEN

Viking warriors longed to be chosen for death in battle by Odin's warrior maidens, the Valkyries. This meant that, instead of going to hell, warriors would experience a glorious afterlife of feasting and fighting in the golden halls of Valhalla. Here they prepare to fight for the gods in the final battle (Ragnarok) of this present world.

White pottery figure of the Aztec lord of death

Sacred sites

THE ICE AGE CAVE pictures of Europe — and their ancient equivalents in Australia, America, and Africa — show us that humankind has always recognized and respected sacred spaces, where the everyday and the eternal meet. Sacred sites may be temporary or permanent, and the same place may be reused many times. Many Christian churches, for instance, are on the sites of pagan temples. Lakes, rivers, caves, woods, or mountaintops may be as spiritual as a temple or church. A place may declare itself sacred simply by its beauty — something the Japanese recognize in erecting *torii* gates (right), in places that are natural shrines. A totem pole, erected to proclaim a family's mythological descent, is also visible proof that the world of humankind and the world of gods and spirits are one and the same.

Most probably an altar, this flat sandstone block was 16 feet (5 meters) long

STANDING STONES

The building of the great Neolithic temple at Stonehenge in Wiltshire, Great Britain, occurred between about 2500 and 1500 B.C. The sacred stones, which are aligned with the sun, moon, and stars, are thought to have had astronomical connections. Stonehenge was also adopted as a sacred site by the druids, Celtic priests of the Iron Age (c. 1100 B.C.).

Curved ends of horizontal bars reach toward heaven

GATEWAYS TO HEAVEN

A *torii* is a gateless entranceway that marks the point where ordinary space becomes sacred space. A *torii* stands at the entrance to each Japanese Shinto shrine, and also in front of the sacred Mount Fuji (right). Because *torii* means bird, it is sometimes said that the *torii* is erected to provide a resting place for birds, so that their song will please the gods at dawn.

Thunderbird makes lightning by opening and closing its eyes

GREAT PYRAMIDS

The Egyptian sun god Ra was born on a pyramid-shaped piece of land jutting out of the primal ocean. This shape was then adopted by the Egyptian pharaohs (kings) for their tombs, putting them under the protection of the sun god.

The thunderbird creates thunder by flapping its wings

Mythical monuments

The totem poles of North American Indians are carved heraldic monuments displaying images of a family's or clan's mythological descent. Sometimes wealthy families commissioned totem poles as memorials to their dead relatives. The Native American Kwakiutl people say that the first totem pole, *kakaluyuwish* (pole that holds up the sky) was made by Wakiash, a Kwakiutl chief, with knowledge that he won from the animal-people when Raven flew him around the world.

This thunderbird totem pole is among the many historical totem poles that stand in Stanley Park in Vancouver, Canada. *Thunderbird* was copied in 1988 from the original, which was erected in 1927.

TEMPLE OF THE MAIDEN

The word "parthenon" means "temple of the maiden," and the Parthenon was the great temple of Athena situated on the Acropolis at Athens, in Greece. Athena, goddess of war and wisdom, was the patron of the city. The Parthenon contained her statue in gold and ivory and a frieze depicting battle scenes and processions of worshipers.

GOLDEN WATERS

Gold was so important to the Incas that they called it the sweat of the sun god Inti. At El Dorado lake (above) in Colombia, each new king was coated in gold dust before sailing out to throw gold offerings into the water. The Spanish conquerors of Peru heard rumors of this and searched in vain for the kingdom of El Dorado and its fabulous riches.

At sunrise and sunset, Uluru displays spectacular shades of orange and purple

MAJESTIC MOUNTAIN

The sacred site of Uluru, or Ayers Rock, rises from the central desert of Australia with great natural majesty. The focus of many myths among the Aborigines of central Australia, Uluru was said to have been built in the Dreamtime by two boys playing with mud after rain.

A human ancestor figure

D-shaped adze

Blade is tied on to the adze with string

CARVING TOOLS

Totem poles are carved with simple tools. First the log is roughly hewn with an elbow adze, and then the animal shapes are roughly defined with a D-shaped adze. Deep-cut details are achieved with curved knives.

Curved knives

Elbow adze

A curved knife is used to add detail to the totem pole

WORKING THE WOOD

Totem poles are usually carved from red cedar, which grows up to 200 feet (60 meters) tall. Carvers work up the pole from the bottom to the top, with the pole lying horizontally on its side. The wood is kept soft by dousing it with pans of hot water.

End of the world

The world will end when the rainbow serpent chews his own tail

COSMIC SERPENT
In West Africa Aido-Hwedo, the rainbow snake, carried the creator in his mouth while the world was made, and then circled around the Earth to hold it together. Red monkeys beneath the sea forge iron bars to feed him. When the iron runs out, Aido-Hwedo will chew his own tail, the world will convulse, and the Earth and all its burdens will slide into the sea.

JUST AS MYTHOLOGIES TELL how the world began, so they predict how it will end, often in a terrible fire or flood. The Aborigines of southeastern Australia believed that the end would come when one of the four props that held up the sky rotted away, allowing the sky to fall. The Native American Cherokee believed that the world was a great floating island, held by four cords hanging down from the sky, and that when these rotted through, the Earth would sink back beneath the sea. The ancient Egyptians, who feared every night that the sun god would be defeated in his journey through the underworld and fail to reappear, also foresaw a time when the god would grow so old and tired that he would forget who he was, so that all he had created would come to an end.

Rocky matter from an explosion in space

The world serpent has many heads

When Brahma awakes, he rises on a lotus flower from the god Vishnu

Lakshmi, Vishnu's wife, the goddess of fortune

At night Vishnu rests on the world serpent, Shesha

END OF THE KALPA
For Hindus, time is an endless cycle of days and nights of Brahma, or kalpas. During the day, when Brahma is awake, the world is created anew; when Brahma goes to sleep, the kalpa ends. Each kalpa lasts 4.32 billion years.

GREAT WORLD POLE

According to the Native American Cheyenne people, the Great White Grandfather Beaver of the North is gnawing the great pole that holds up the world. When he gnaws right through, the world will end. The Tsimshian of the northwest coast say that the pole on which the world spins is held up by Amala. He has a servant who gives him strength by rubbing his back with wild-duck oil once a year. The oil is nearly used up; when it runs out, Amala will die, and the world will fall.

North American family totem (symbol) of the beaver

Aztec calendar stone c. 1352

MYTH OF THE FIVE SUNS

The Aztecs believed that this world was the fifth, and that each creation had its own sun. The fifth sun first shone on August 13, 3114 B.C., and will last until at least A.D. 4772. But it will not last forever, for "all moons, all years, all days, all winds, reach their completion and pass away."

The Sun god Ra in the guise of a cat

Apep, the chaos serpent

EGYPTIAN APEP

Each night, as the sun god Ra voyaged through the underworld, his ship was attacked by the chaos serpent Apep, his mortal enemy. If Apep ever devoured Ra, the world would end. Each night Ra took the form of a cat and cut off Apep's head.

THE BIG CRUNCH

Many mythologies envisage a cycle of creation and destruction and foresee the emergence of a new world after this one ends. According to scientific theory, this is perfectly feasible. The universe, which is currently expanding, may one day reach a maximum size and collapse in on itself in a "Big Crunch." The matter and energy from the collapsed universe may then bounce back to create a new universe.

Midgard serpent — monstrous child of the trickster Loki

LAST BATTLE OF THE NORSE GODS

The warlike Vikings thought the world would end in a final cataclysmic battle, in which all the main gods would die and the Earth would be consumed by fire. This battle is Ragnarok, the twilight of the gods. The wolf Fenrir, child of the trickster Loki, will break his bonds, kill Odin the all-father, and swallow the sun. But from this world's ruin, a new creation will arise.

Index

Acknowledgments

Dorling Kindersley would like to thank:
Alan Hills, Philip Nicholls, Christi Graham, John Williams, Kevin Lovelock, Jim Rossiter, and Janet Peckham of the British Museum, London; Kalamandalam Vijayakumar and Kalamandalam Barbara Vijayakumar; and the African Crafts Centre, Covent Garden, London.
Photography: Andy Crawford
Researcher: Robert Graham
Index: Chris Bernstein
Design assistance: Jill Bunyan and Anna Martin

Picture credits:
The publisher would like to thank the following for their kind permission to reproduce the photographs.
t=top, b=bottom, a=above, c=center, l=left, r=right

AKG London: 39tr, 39l; Boymans van Beuningen Museum, Rotterdam *The Tower of Babel*, Pieter Brueghel the Elder 9r; Erich Lessing/Württembergisches Landesmuseum, Stuttgart 9bc, 26tl, 46tl; SMPK Kupferstichkabinett, Berlin 14tl; Torquil Cramer 58/59c; Universitets Oldsaksamling, Oslo 34bc; Von der Heydt Museum, Wuppertal *Flora, Awakening Flowers*, 1876, by Arnold Bucklin (1827–1901) 25bl; **American Museum of Natural History:** 43br, 50tr, 52cl; Thos. Beiswenger 41r; **Ancient Art & Architecture Collection:** D.F. Head 31tr; Ronald Sheridan 10bl, 13br, 23cl, 26br, 27ar, 45l, 45ca;

Ashmolean Museum, Oxford: 16c, 32br, 42/43c; **Duncan Baird Publishers Archive:** 16tl; Japanese Gallery 11cr, 33c; **Bildarchiv Preußischer Kulturbesitz:** 34tl; SMPK Berlin 18; Staatliche Museum, Berlin 48tr; **Bridgeman Art Library, London/New York:** British Museum, London *The Weighing of the Heart Against Maat's Feather of Truth*, Egyptian, early 19th Dynasty, c.1300 B.C., *Book of the Dead of the Royal Scribe* 54br; By Courtesy of the Board of the Trustees of the V&A *Vishnu in the Center of his Ten Avatars*, Jaipur area, 18th century 20tl; Galleria degli Uffizi, Florence, Italy *The Birth of Venus*, c.1485, by Sandro Botticelli (1444/5–1510) 42cl; Louvre, Paris, France/Giraudon *Stele of a Woman before Re-Harakhy*, Egyptian, c.1000BC 15tl; Musée Condé, Chantilly, France MS 860/401 f.7 *The Story of Adam and Eve*, detail from "Cas des Nobles Hommes et Femmes" by Boccaccio, translated by Laurent de Premierfait, French 1465, *Works of Giovanni Boccaccio* (1313–75) 9bl (right), 17br; Museo Correr, Venice, Italy *Glimpse of Hell* (panel) by Flemish School (15th century) 55bl; Piazza della Signoria, Florence/Lauros – Giraudon *Perseus with the Head of a Medusa*, 1545–54, in the Loggia dei Lanzi, by Benvenuto Cellini (1500–71) 35bcr; Private Collection Genesis 6:11-24 Noah's Ark, Nuremberg Bible (Biblia Sacra Germanaica), 1483 21cb; **British Museum, London:** 6br, 6bl, 9bc, 13tr, 14tr, 16r, 17c, 17tr, 17r, 18tr, 19r, 23t, 25tl, 28bl, 31br, 35tr, 36c, 38br, 39bc, 42tl, 43tc, 43tr, 52bl, 53tl; **Cambridge Museum of**

Anthropology: 21r, 57tr; **Central Art Archives:** The Old Students House, Helsinki 19tl; **Jean-Loup Charmet:** 9tr, 21tl; **Christie's Images:** *In the Well of the Great Wave of Kanagawa*, c.1797, by Hokusai Katsushika (1760–1849) 20/21b, 30r, 31l; **Bruce Coleman Ltd:** Jeff Foott Productions 44tl; **CM Dixon:** 31bc; **Edimedia:** 14cr; **AKG London:** 33l; British Library Or 13805 56bl; Freer Gallery of Art 24br; Victoria & Albert Museum, London 12/13c; **Mary Evans Picture Library:** 12bl, 12br, 23bl, 28c, 30tl, 32bl; **Werner Forman Archive:** Anthropology Museum, Veracruz University, Jalapa 55r; Arhus Kunstmuseum, Denmark 32cl; Dallas Museum of Art 28bl; David Bernstein Fine Art, New York 51r; Field Museum of Natural History, Chicago 11t; Museum of the American Indian, Heye Foundation 15cl; Smithsonian Institution 14bl; State Museum of Berlin 18cl; **Glasgow Museums (St Mungo):** 33bl, 34bl, 40bl, 50br, 54tr; **Hamburgisches Museum für Völkerkunde:** 45tr; **Robert Harding Picture Library:** Patrick Mathews 54bl; **Michael Holford:** British Museum 9cr (below), 10bc, 10tl, 15bl, 16bl, 42bl, 57cr; Kunisada 15br; Museum of Mankind 44bl; Victoria & Albert Museum, London 11br; **Hutchison Library:** Ian Lloyd 59br; **Images Colour Library:** 26c, 57br, 58tr; Impact: Mark Henley 59cr; **INAH/Michael Zabe:** 21tc, 24l, 18bc; **Barnabas Kindersley:** 55tl, 55c (above); **MacQuitty International Photo Collection:** 41bl; **The Board of Trustees of the National Museums & Galleries on Merseyside:** 30bl, 53tr; **Nilesh Mistry:** 32tl; **Musée de L'Homme, France:** 22l; D Ponsard 38l, 56l; **Museum of Anthropology, Vancouver:** 59cl; **Museum of Mankind:** 6cl, 34c, 37tc; **National Maritime**

Museum: 4c, 49tr; **National Museum of Copenhagen:** 36/37b; **Natural History Museum,** London: 4tcl, 29tr, 29c, 48/49b, 48tl, 49tl, 49r; © David Neel, 1998: 4tl; Peter Newark's Pictures: 8br, 18r, 41cl, 51c; **Panos Pictures:** Caroline Penn 59bl; **Ann & Bury Peerless:** 22cl, 47tl; **Pitt Rivers Museum, Oxford:** 8bcl, 12tr, 25cr, 40tr 53bl; **Planet Earth Pictures:** Jan Tove Johansson 10l; **Axel Poignant Archive:** 13cl, 23br, 37tl; **Rex Features:** Tim Brooke 55bcl; **Rijksmuseum voor Volkenkunde:** 22r; **Réunion des Musées Nationaux Agence Photographique:** Hervé Lewandowski 28tl, 35cr; **Richard Lambert** 39cbr; **Science Photo Library:** Chris Bjornberg 10/11c; Sally Benusen (1982) 56/57c; **South American Pictures:** Tony Morrison 15tr, 59cr; **Spectrum Colour Library:** 58cr; **Statens Historika Museum, Stockholm:** 9br; **Oliver Strewe:** 52cr; 31cra.

Jacket: American Museum of Natural History: front cl; Ancient Art & Architecture Collection: front tl, back tl; Ronald Sheridan inside front cr, back cr; **Ashmolean Museum, Oxford:** back bl; Duncan Baird Publishers Archive: inside front tl; **Bildarchiv Preußischer Kulturbesitz:** State Museum Berlin front c; **British Museum, London:** front tc, bc, back tc, bc; **Danish National Museum, Copenhagen:** inside front b; **Werner Forman Archive:** State Museum Berlin, front tr, back tr; **Hamburgisches Museum für Völkerkunde:** inside front cl; **Michael Holford:** front tcr, back tcr; **Natural History Museum, London:** front r, back cla; **Ann & Bury Peerless:** back cra; **Axel Poignant Archive:** back br; **Statens Historika Museum, Stockholm:** front tr, back tr.